# Adventures from the Edge

*How a Quintessential Wife and Mother Morphed into a Free and Independent Warrior Marching Through Life with Awe and Wonder*

## Carol Vance Edwards

Fulton Books, Inc.
Meadville, PA

Published by Fulton Books 2020

ISBN 978-1-64654-675-6 (paperback)
ISBN978-1-64654-676-3 (digital)

Printed in the United States of America

# Contents

# Reflection

## A Mother's Advice

Do not live with a troubled heart
Rather, greet each dawn
With a happy plan
And do the very best you can
Do not feel rejection
When others do not share your point of view
Perhaps they hear a different drummer
And do what they must do
You stay on the righteous path
And God will see you through

—Jenet Watters Vance, 1987

To Rebekah,

Come travel with me !

Enjoy the trip !

Carol Vance Edwards

2022

Jenet Watters Vance
1914–1992

# Expect the Unexpected

"Don't you daahaa land theyha, that's a Nicaraguan drug-runnin' strip!" my Alabama friend shouted to the pilot. We were on our way from Guatemala City to the Atlantic Coast for the weekend. My friend, Robin, had invited a guest, Maureen, and me to spend some time with them at their home on Lake Isabal (*isa ball*), part of the Rio Dulce river system. The sudden downdrafts that day were more than this little family had ever experienced on the forty-five-minute commute to their lake house. Guatemala is about the size of Ohio, with over thirty active, inactive, and dormant volcanoes. It was a topography not conducive to emergency landings. After the third or fourth alarming punch earthward, Maureen became not only alarmed, not only frightened, but actually catatonic. Her eyes glazed over, and she was totally unresponsive. This, the brave bubbly lady I met on the *Queen Elizabeth II* who was touring Europe alone.

That set the stage for the pilot's curt announcement that we were "going down." The sky was purple and churning. The lake had white caps. Panic permeated the air in that little plane. We landed on the only clearing in the jungle. Taxiing to the end of the runway, we saw that this primitive airstrip concealed a small two-story cinder block building. It *was* a drug-running strip. Knowing that being there was not only trespassing but very dangerous, we were anxious to get back in the air. The storm passed quickly. We took off as fast as we could just as six mounted men, brandishing rifles, followed by a pack of barking dogs, were practically nipping at our heels.

This wasn't exactly what my dear friend Maureen was expecting when she accepted the invitation from the comfort of her Long Island living room. We had met a year before on a cruise to England aboard the *Queen Elizabeth II* and bonded immediately. She had just retired and was beginning a European grand tour by herself. We ultimately became good friends and traveled together again after she was back in the states. Now, I was an administrator at the largest, private, bilingual school in Guatemala and Maureen was planning to visit me.

Robin and Steve ask me to join them on Lake Isabal and extended the invitation to my visitor. Little Madeline was in second grade at the American School, and that was how I met her parents. Expatriates are generally a lively, interesting bunch of people and they tend to gravitate together. This wild adventure wasn't exactly what I had signed on for either, but living in a foreign country is full of surprises.

This was the exciting start to our tranquil respite on the beautiful Rio Dulce *(Sweet Water)* area of Eastern Guatemala. Maureen's two-week stay had all the elements of a wonderful vacation. She referred to this portion of her Central American experience and our trip to Monterrico as her "Indiana Jones" chapters. The calmer chapters were full of ruins, gourmet food, and shopping. My weekends continued to be full of new experiences, helping my staff discover and appreciate this beautiful country and travel, travel, travel. Exploring Guatemala was not for the faint of heart. The most adventurous among us soon learned—expect the unexpected.

# The Metamorphosis
# Begins

# Beginning My Other Life

In terms of timelines, I define my life in three segments: my "other life," the "single years," and the "here and now." My other life was very comfortable. I had a new home, a vacation cottage, two grown children, and a husband I loved. And then, my world came crashing down, and I was like a middle-aged Alice in Wonderland. But before I describe my descent into the rabbit hole, let me give you a more detailed description of the woman I was.

My friends called me Donna Reed. Donna was the star of a popular 1960s television show, where she played the quintessential wife, mother, housekeeper. One of my peers even bought me a Donna Reed watch! If I wasn't teaching, which I loved, I was making clothes for my daughter and me. If I wasn't sewing, I was cooking or gardening or writing. I had written several cookbooks on the preparation of wild game that my husband—and then, my son—proudly brought home. I was invited to join several outdoor writing organizations, which greatly impacted my writing career. Then my friend, Angie, and I became established as itinerant lecturers on cruise ships, teaching arts and crafts. This was an exciting new chapter I was eager to pursue. If I wasn't smiling, I was sleeping. I loved my life. I was happy.

All that changed, however, when my marriage of twenty-eight years fell apart. My life fell apart. All I held near and dear had been shattered by deceit, lies, and infidelity. Teaching became my life. I threw myself into every project and unit of study. The classroom became my world. As a result of one of these projects, my class made a large contribution to the Pearl S. Buck Foundation, which was close to our school district. I was invited to attend the Buck annual meeting, where representatives of the foundation from around the world came together. As a result of that meeting, I was offered a position in the largest, private, bi-lingual school in Guatemala. In order to get away from an ugly divorce, I jumped at the opportunity to leave heartbreak behind. I leaped into the "rabbit hole" and accepted an offer for a guest and me to visit Guatemala. We were encouraged to make a list of things we would like to see after a tour of the campus and a formal interview.

My friend, neighbor, fellow teacher, and I pored over *National Geographic* magazines, looking for as much information on Guatemala as we could find. We hurriedly made the necessary travel arrangements and flew to Guatemala over our Easter break. The founder and director of the American School met us at the airport and took us to a beautiful hotel close to the campus. Our first hurdle there in that Latin American country was over breakfast our first morning. The menu was in Spanish. While I studied the words, looking for context clues, Mildred ordered first—in Spanish! Her high school language classes kicked in, and she did quite well. And she got a lot of practice on this trip. After an intensive interview with several administrators, we toured the five-acre campus. We were very impressed with the beautiful amenities this institution had to offer. From kindergarten right through postgraduate work, this was a modern beautiful facility. I began to believe I could do this.

Each morning, a Suburban was waiting outside the Casa Grande Hotel to take us on the day's excursion. Our translator, Rosa Lillia, and the chauffeur were proud to show us the grandeur of their country. It was so exciting to experience the lush Central American landscape and its incredible climate. This small country has the distinction of being accessible to both the Atlantic and Pacific Oceans. We walked the volcanic black-sand beaches of the Pacific coast and marveled at the ancient ruins. We soaked in the intensity of the almost equatorial sun and relished the crisp, cool nights. What a paradise! And to add drama to the whole tableau, an active volcano lit up the tropical darkness with rivers of vibrant red and orange lava cascading down the side of Volcan Pacaya, every night.

But perhaps the most breathtaking day of our visit was the Easter celebration and parades in the ancient capital of Antigua. La Antigua has been declared a Monument of the Americas and a World Heritage site. The former capital of the Mayan world was practically destroyed by a strong earthquake in 1773. More than fifty churches, convents, and palaces dating from the sixteenth to the eighteenth centuries make La Antigua one of the America's most beautiful cities. The architecture is beyond impressive. It is magnificent. The cathedrals, monasteries, and convents are all in different stages of disrepair. Bougainvillea vines grace the stone arches and whitewashed walls with their vibrant purple and crimson blooms, everywhere. Three different traditions come together in today's Guatemala: the pre-Columbian world of the Maya, the Spanish colonial heritage, and a modern forward-looking society. This diversity is central to the country and has great appeal as a tourist destination. It has been said that Holy Week in La Antigua, Guatemala, is even more spectacular than in Spain. Hundreds of men and women carry immense and beautifully carved mahogany floats bearing colonial statues of Jesus, Mary, and the saints through the streets. Participants walk on ornate pictures painstakingly made of flowers, seeds, and sawdust to honor the religious figures. Some are dressed in ornate costumes and parody the Spanish invaders. It was an unprecedented display. We were so fortunate to be visiting during this spectacular religious holiday. The whole visit was almost surreal. It was liberating. It was empowering. It was exhilarating. It was going to be the next chapter in my life.

By the end of this amazing visit, with Mildred's help, I had decided to accept if a position at the American School of Guatemala was offered to me. Several days after arriving home, I was offered the position of resource teacher. It was a new position created just for me. Rather than give me a classroom assignment, it was decided that I could have more positive influence in the educational curriculum if I were able to observe, motivate, advise, and guide the staff as needed. It was a perfect fit for me. So perfect, that in just a few months, I was asked to become the principal of the English curriculum at the lower school (K–6).

The famous Santa Catalina Arch in Antigua

Antigua, Guatemala's Colonial Splendor
seen from the center square

Easter week Procession in Guatemala's Ancient capital, Antigua

My job at the American School of Guatemala in Guatemala City would start in July. As what would be my last year in the classroom came to a close, a friend and I were planning a trip to the Mediterranean. Pat Marino and I traveled well together. We taught crafts well together. We had worked for a number of years in the same school district, and she was my children's kindergarten teacher. We were both recently divorced, our children were grown, and we both felt that now, it was time for us. We were spreading our wings and taking advantage of the wonderful opportunity cruising afforded us.

Our itinerary for this trip included Italy, Greece, Yugoslavia/ Croatia, and Turkey. I was moving out of my apartment, scattering my possessions all over northeast Pennsylvania and packing for two destinations—this amazing cruise and the move to Guatemala. The farewell assembly the last day of school was poignant. Two of my friends "signed" the Whitney Houston song, "That's What Friends Are For." They were dressed in black, wore white gloves and with only a black light on their hands, all that was visible in the darkened multipurpose room were those white hands signing the words as the whole school sang that beautiful goodbye to me.

> Keep smilin', keep shinin'
> Knowing you can always count on me, for sure
> That's what friends are for
> For good times and bad times
> I'll be on your side forever more
> That's what friends are for…

Wow! It was a complete surprise, and I was overwhelmed. There weren't too many dry eyes in that room as everyone waved goodbye. While the last notes of the song were still echoing in my head, our hired car pulled up to the school, full of suitcases and Pat. We were off to catch the red-eye flight to Rome. It was a wonderful trip. We tried to see all Rome had to offer, but we only scratched the surface of that sprawling city. We enjoyed Venice, had a lunch of octopus in

Hvar, Croatia, reveled in the biblical city of Ephesis, then the Greek Islands and Istanbul. What an amazing itinerary. I had been poring over the list of possible excursions in the Greek Islands and became very interested in the island of Santorini.

# Santorini

The town of Santorini is perched on top of a very steep cliff, with access to the sea on one side and a convoluted cobblestone street on the other side, navigated by donkeys. We loved the village and bought some wonderful things—cable knit sweaters for my grandsons, among them. Then we came to the donkey trail leading down to the sea. Pat was eager to ride down on a donkey, but I opted to walk down the steep slopes between hairpin turns. Hoofed animals and I never got along. Wearing fashionable shoes, trying not to slip on the cobblestones, and avoiding the donkey road apples proved to be too much. Halfway down, I gave up and allowed a little Greek man to lead me to a set of steps. I had noticed the steps strategically spaced on my walk down and wondered about them. They were to allow people like me who decided to ride the donkeys after all. I climbed the stairs and mounted the little animal. It wasn't long before I caught up with Pat, and I was really enjoying the ride. Rather than take the cable car, we decided to ride back up. At the top of the cliff, we decided to ride back down! Needless to say, walking on the ship the next day was painful and laborious. Our legs were screaming for days.

We absolutely loved the Greek islands. They were more beautiful than we ever imagined. The color of the Mediterranean was an intense blue and the villages an incredible white, white. The contrast was spectacular. In Santorini, a beautiful clear sky showcased the village houses, adding another dimension to an already awesome landscape. I wanted to return.

# Turkey and Ukraine

After Santorini and Greece, Pat and I were bombarded with antiquity, ruins, and history. Terms like mosques, bazaars, Tokopki, Delphi, Ephesus, and the temple of Artemis swirled around in our heads and peppered the brochures extolling one excursion after another. We were headed up the Sea of Marmara to Istanbul, a city that separates Europe from Asia. Marmara is purportedly the smallest sea on the globe. It provided a much-needed respite from the splendors and ruins of Greece, the island of Hvar, and the port of Dubrovnik, Croatia. Concentrating on our classes, Pat and I submerged ourselves in arts and crafts and enjoyed the company of our fellow passengers. We were entering a part of the world that neither of us had ever dreamed of experiencing. In the beginning of this cruise, we took pride in calculating the monetary exchange rate and paying for things in the local currency. By the port of Kusadasi, we had given up and instead just held out some money and let the vendors/salespeople take what was fair!

Kusadasi is at the southern end of the Sea of Marmara. It is close to the home of the Virgin Mary and the ancient city of Ephesus. Ephesus is supposedly built on the place known for the Oracle of Delphi. Pat and I chose a bus trip to that ancient city. The guide was very fluent in English and gave us a wonderful background of the area during our trip up the mountain. At one point, he asked if there were any questions. I was still an active member of outdoor writers organizations, and I inquired about wild game in Turkey. As an answer, he asked me to meet him once we got back into town.

He was a realtor and took us to his office to finish up some business. While we were there, a parade came down the street. We got really excited. No one else saw this unique, very Turkish parade down the main street in the middle of town, and we felt very privileged to be there. Next, our guide took us to a beautiful restaurant right on the water, with our ship in the background. He told the waiter to bring a sampling of everything from the menu. Then we talked business. I was trying to see if a Turkish hunt would be possible and profitable. We exchanged information and made plans to stay in touch. While hunts are booked for wild boar, ibex, red deer, and chamois, nothing ever came of this venture, however. He sent us off to visit his brother at the local market, where we were invited to a cup of Turkish tea while we shopped. I'm sure Pat and I undoubtedly had a more interesting afternoon and evening than anyone else on the ship.

I'll never forget waking up to see incredible minarets and domed mosques punctuating the skyline outside our window. It was breathtaking, and a huge dose of reality that we really were experiencing this area of the world. Istanbul was also known as Constantinople and Byzantium. The six minarets at the Blue Mosque, were commanding, but entering this place of worship was awesome. We placed our shoes in a plastic bag and donned a head covering to cover our hair. There were no pews. Men knelt on a profusion of beautiful red carpets, and a hush hung over that huge place of worship, the many beautiful blue glass windows casting an ethereal glow, which added to the mystical, spiritual aura. To be truthful, I was so moved at being there and experiencing what Sultan Ahmet built in the seventeenth century, that I became emotional. This was a dramatic introduction to the rest of day.

The Haga Sophia was the residence and administrative headquarters for the Ottoman sultans and was equally impressive as was the Temple of Artemis, one of the seven wonders of the ancient world. My favorite, however, was the Tokopki Seraglio Museum. Getting up close and personal with the accoutrements of life in the fifteenth century transported us back in time. What a counterpoint to life in the twentieth century! We ended our day with a visit to the Grand Bazaar. The Grand Bazaar is a shopper's paradise—a cacophony of sights and sounds. I have a magnificent small carpet that I splurged on, and is a beautiful reminder of that full day in Istanbul.

The ship proceeded into the Black Sea. Our next port of call—the city of Odessa, Russia. This pivotal port was founded by decree of Catherine the Great in 1794. It has connections with Ancient Greece, the Ottoman Empire, and the Russian Revolution. It is now part of Ukraine. For the first time on this cruise, I was uncomfortable. We had to surrender our passports to a Russian officer at the end of the gangplank. Backed by a group of armed soldiers standing at attention, we were only allowed on Russian soil after handing over that most precious document. In return, we got a card with a number on it. When we returned to the ship, we could redeem that number for our passports. A little scary in 1990, but thankfully, there was no problem on our return. Our lunch was incredible. Eight bottles of liquor lined the end of each table. Course after course appeared, all delicious. However, the bottles remained untouched, clearly a clash of cultures. Was the perception of Americans that of heavy drinkers, or was drinking hard liquor at lunch part of theirs? Interesting. Folkloric dancers took the stage in magnificent costumes and gave us a musical tour of their country's sights and sounds. Again, I was overwhelmed. Tears of joy spilled down my cheeks as I savored this look into the fierce culture of Asia's Russia and Ukraine. It was breathtaking. We walked around the beautiful and famous opera house and then stopped at one of the most commanding destinations of the tour—The White Palace. With its rich history and strategic location, it is often referred to as the "Pearl of the Black Sea." The palace, designed by Nikolay Krasnov in 1911, is in the Renaissance style and the grounds were very impressive and meticulously maintained. Odessa is the third largest city in the Ukrainian Soviet Socialist Republic. It is an ice-free port, home to a fishing fleet and the Seventh-Kilometer Market, the largest of its kind in Europe. This was just the appetizer, however, for the main course to come—Yalta.

Disembarking the next day at Yalta, the passenger behind me leaned forward and whispered, "Are you going to cry today too?" I didn't think anyone noticed as I surreptitiously wiped away yesterday's tears. The history, splendor, and topography of the Black Sea region was amazing to me. I think I was on cognitive overload, having experienced all the splendors the Mediterranean ports had to

The Opera House, in Odessa, Ukraine

offer, and now this. It began to be too much. I am a history buff and admittedly, running my fingers through a surveyor's mark made by George Washington in a stone wall, or touching the wood of Abraham Lincoln's cabin gave me a thrill, but nothing could compare to being in the same room and seeing the actual table where Stalin, Churchill, and Roosevelt met on February fourth to the eleventh, 1945. History was made at that meeting, while discussing Germany and Europe's postwar reorganization. I didn't cry, but I was awed and moved to be in this place at this time. Interestingly enough, Roosevelt stayed at the Palace of Livadia, Churchill at the Vorontsov Palace, and Stalin at the Yusupov Palace. Ukraine, a region obviously steeped in history, a region of palaces and a wild past, were all very foreign and exotic to us tourists from the other side of the world. This resort city was founded by Catherine the Great on the site of the Turkish Khadzhibel Fortress. It has been called a Landmark of Modern History by the Seven Wonders of the Ukraine project. When I was young, I don't think I ever heard of Ukraine. Now we were immersed in the history, architecture, and antiquities of the region. Travel is truly enlightening and educational.

To put all this in perspective, the history of our country goes only back to the years prior to 1776. I remember feeling the same way after the third day at Williamsburg. As much as I enjoyed history, I was becoming satiated. And I was satiated now. Ahead of us was a stop at Varna Bulgaria, then back through the Sea of Marmara, the Aegean Sea, with the cruise ending in Rome. Rome! Having been immersed in history dating back to the fourteenth century was, for us, mind-boggling. We just don't have that kind of history in our country. We were awed and incredulous. I really needed the respite the days at sea would give us. I looked forward to concentrating on teaching arts and crafts and clearing my mind, and I think Pat felt the same.

We were agog in Rome. You turn a corner, and wow there's the Colosseum! Right in the middle of town. Pat had studied the brochures and gathered as much information as she could on this ancient city. She really wanted to see the Catacombs, so that was added to our list. Rome also marked the end of our cruise. After several days in a quaint hotel, we turned our eyes and hearts homeward.

And so then, I had only a few days to pack, repack, and prepare to move to Guatemala. What was I thinking? As I started my tenure in Guatemala, ruin after ruin dating back decades came to the fore. I had no idea what overload was! For the next almost three years, the culture and ancient structures of the Maya civilization permeated my life. Eventually, I relaxed and the old curiosity returned. But that was quite a summer. Ruins, ruins, ruins.

# A Day in Cozumel

Mildred and I decided to travel together again sometime. We had so much fun in Guatemala, that we thought it would be nice to take a cruise to the Caribbean and Mexico. Mildred and I taught together in a small rural school in the Lehigh Valley of Pennsylvania, for several years. We ultimately became neighbors outside of Coopersburg, Pennsylvania, and eventually, single women. Mildred was able to travel more than me as she had retired several years before her husband passed away. I was still teaching. I had just separated from my husband and was not looking forward to my first Thanksgiving alone.

Over the years, our home had become the traditional family gathering place for my favorite holiday. I loved giving thanks for all we had and for our wonderful family without the stress and hoopla of Christmas. I also loved planning meals for the entire holiday as relatives arrived and children returned home from college. On Thanksgiving Eve, I always made a hearty squash-and-sausage soup served out of a big fresh pumpkin "tureen." In school after we read about the first Thanksgiving, the children made men and women Pilgrims for place cards for their families, and I made them too! I was always so excited that I was famous, or maybe infamous, for setting the table a week ahead! I wanted to select what serving dishes to use, make sure the glasses were sparkling, the tablecloth without a wrinkle, and decide who would sit where. I loved to place the twenty plus guests strategically around the table to encourage lively conversation. And my Pilgrims always marched up and down the long table, directing relatives to their seats. I was very strong on tradition, and looking for their seats became one of ours.

I started as far ahead as possible on the preparation of the feast, as I didn't get home from work until the Wednesday afternoon before the big day. Breads were baked, pies ready to assemble, onions creamed, sweet potatoes swimming in syrup—I even made the mashed potatoes the day before. With this prologue, understanding my emotional ties to Thanksgiving is evident. Facing this holiday without extended family was tearing me apart.

That's when Millie and I decided to hit the road and ride the waves to Mexico! Getting away was the perfect solution. We sailed out of New Orleans on a sunny afternoon, and the adventure began. It is really quite a distance, about eighty-two miles as the crow flies, down the Mississippi from the port of New Orleans to the open waters of the Gulf of Mexico. That first evening, two seats at our table were empty. We were told that the couple assigned to those seats had missed the sailing, and would be joining us later that evening. Later that evening? What a strange bit of information, as there were no scheduled stops along the river. After dinner Mildred and I were out on the deck, enjoying the night air when we felt the ship slow down. Something was happening. It wasn't long before we saw a tugboat with very bright flood lights pull up alongside our vessel. When the two crafts were moving at exactly the same speed, an apparatus or bundle of straps was lowered to the tug. We watched paralyzed with fear as a woman was strapped into that bundle and slowly began her ascent up the moving ship to the waiting arms of several officers on the closest open deck. Incredibly enough, that performance was repeated as her husband joined her. Those events seemed to set the stage for a cruise full of adventures. It certainly set the stage for conversation at our second dinner!

We were headed for the island of Cozumel, twelve miles off the coast of the Yucatan Peninsula and part of the state of Quintana Roo, across from Playa del Carmen. Cozumel is an island paradise, with everything the beautiful Caribbean has to offer. The island is thirty-four miles long and eleven miles wide. Of course, I wanted to see it all! After much persuasion, Millie agreed to renting a car. The gentleman behind the desk was most polite and eager to put us in a Volkswagen.

Everything was going well until he asked for my driver's license. After much debate, we left our wallets on the ship, taking only bathing suits, a camera, and some money ashore. We were at a stalemate. He needed my license, and I didn't have it with me. We had taken a tender ashore, so going back to the ship would involve waiting for the next tender, and then waiting again to tender back. Most of our precious time on the island would be taken up... Finally, in desperation, he asked if I knew my driver's license number. My number? Oh, my number. Hmmm. I suddenly realized that if I came up with a number, any number, we may be in luck. So I rattled off numbers at random, hoping I had given him the correct amount of digits. Success! He had me sign a form and handed me the keys. We were off! It was a straight-shift car, and the distance between gears was miniscule compared to larger cars that I was used to. After several jerky stops and starts we were off on the road around the island. Mildred, it turned out, was terrified. She had read too much about Mexican police and Mexican jails, and she was sure this was not going to end well. But it did. We had a lovely trip.

We stopped at the famous Chankanaab Beach where we rented snorkel equipment. After several choking and sputtering and coughing fits, we were able to enjoy the beauty that this Caribbean paradise was hiding underwater. Big schools of yellow tail fish swam over and under us, brushing our bodies and obscuring our view. We lingered for too long and reveling in the underwater splendor.

Driving the island loop was beautiful, and we stopped at a lovely hotel to enjoy a lunch poolside with live entertainment. A stop at the shopping mecca downtown rounded out our tour of this tropical island. What a day! Reviewing the highlights of the past few hours made our wait in line for the last tender fly by. As we approached the ship, it became evident that the seas had become rough. The further we went, the rougher it got. Finally, we reached the ship's open portal where a group of officers had gathered. The tender was, at this point, rocking up and down quite vigorously as fellow shipmates were in line with their bags of souvenirs. Anxiety was growing as we watched the portal rise above our heads, and then dip below view. The decision was made to board us from the other side of the ship.

As we proceeded to the other side, the gravity of the situation became obvious. On the other side, the seas were equally as rough. The same scene prevailed. The portal went above us and then below us.

By this time the officers were visibly upset, and we could see that several proposals were on the table as to how to get us aboard. Suddenly, as the portal came down level with the tender, on its way down into the trough of the next wave, an officer jumped into our tender. Timing the waves, he began to count. Officers on the landing dock were waiting to receive passengers. Purchases and bags were dropped. Silence prevailed as this dangerous and daring attempt to get us on board unfolded. Finally, we were instructed to jump on command. The first few brave souls did just that and made it into the arms of the awaiting crew.

Mildred was ten years older than I, and I was very worried about her making it to the ship. One by one, each of us took a leap of blind faith, responding to the repeated shouts of "Go"! Amazingly enough they got all of us aboard safely. I have no idea how they managed to get that tender up out of the choppy sea to its place hanging tethered to the side of the ship. Packages and purses were distributed once we were all safely aboard. You could feel the stress of those brave men begin to dissipate as the portal was closed and the officers resumed their duties.

What had begun as an innocuous visit to an island paradise turned out to be a day full of excitement and adventure. We were two tired old teachers that night! Expect the unexpected.

# Meeting Maureen

Cruising helped Mildred cope with the loss of her husband. Cruising helped Angie, Pat and me cope with failed marriages and downsized lifestyles. There's nothing like a vacation to exciting countries to lift one's spirits. And we were all determined to keep our spirits lifted! Mildred was retired, so she was able to take even more advantage of this amazing opportunity that Angie had stumbled on. Angie went first, and then became my strength, my mentor, and my cruise partner for a number of years. We shared supplies and ideas and used our summer vacations and holidays to get away. What a wonderful way to see the world. And see the world we did—or a great deal of it.

My daughter, Karen, was getting married in August, and I was giving them their honeymoon—a cruise to Bermuda, teaching arts and crafts. To do an "orientation," Karen and I sailed to Bermuda in June, and I booked another cruise there in August for she and her new husband, Tom. Angie and I booked a crossing on the *Queen Elizabeth II* at the same time. Boarding different ships in New York City harbor the day after the wedding was very special. Coincidentally, our ships were in the same double berth! As soon as we were settled in, we raced to the top deck, so we could wave goodbye as the honeymooners left the harbor and headed down the Hudson River and out to sea. Bermuda, here we come!

Angie and I were headed to Southampton, England. It was a huge ship and very British. High tea was served at four every day by white-gloved waiters, the public rooms were lavishly decorated with gorgeous floral arrangements, and there was a separate dining room for the first-class passengers. This was 1990. How times have changed! We always asked for second seating, and we always requested a large table in order to meet new people. At dinner that first night, we got to know our table mates and were soon exchanging stories. The woman next to me related that she was an elementary school principal, and when she turned sixty, she hired a helicopter to take her to school, landing on the playground to her students' delight. This was her first cruise, and she was visiting relatives in Ireland before embarking on a tour of Europe, by herself, to celebrate her retirement. As the evening unfolded, I was certain that this bubbly independent lady would become another lifetime friend. And she did.

Angie, Maureen, and I delighted in the lively dinner conversations each night and spent all our evenings together. When we parted, it was with a promise to stay in touch. After we docked, I got the news that my first grandson had been born. I called my son, Scott, immediately, and cried softly in that cramped English telephone booth as my son lovingly described his newborn son.

Angie and I explored Southampton, went to the Isle of Wight, took a double-deck bus tour of London, and even went to Buckingham Palace and Westminster Abbey, before rejoining the ship for the return voyage. We were home a week when one of my agents called. They had a cancellation, and could I board a ship in three days bound for Bermuda? Sure, I could. I always had the craft bag stocked and ready. I called Maureen, explained the last-minute booking, and invited her to join me. When, she wanted to know. Wednesday was the answer. You could probably hear the scream all over Long Island as she hung up. The phone rang a few minutes later, and that began the Maureen and Carol travel odyssey.

On these cruises, we were always treated like passengers. We always ate in the dining room. We always enjoyed the entertainment. We were able to book tours in every port of call and enjoy the excitement of each locale. Our classes were only scheduled for the days at sea. All this in return for a minimal agent fee per person. Certainly, a huge deal and one that provided the opportunity to travel on an incredibly low budget. Frequent-flier miles helped with airfare when we needed to fly to a ship. So, my lifestyle was not too damaged.

I managed to turn around what could have been a depressing and uneventful period in my life into an exciting and colorful one. And meeting Angie and me had a profound effect on Maureen's retirement. Her children never knew where she was off to next!

# Adventures in Guatemala

# First Visitors

I went to Guatemala in July 1990. By August I was settled in. I met a vivacious and energetic woman at a school seminar. Dorothy Aquinos was from Philadelphia, owned a private secretarial school, and was a concert pianist. She was tall, blond, and stunningly attractive, in a Carol Channing sort of way. I was instantly drawn to her outgoing personality. One evening someone was knocking on my apartment door. I was in bed reading and very startled by this intrusion. It was Dorothy. She ordered me to get dressed and announced that we were going to an art-gallery opening. "I want to introduce you to some friends," she said. A night out! The gallery was only a block from my apartment in the Zona Viva, or the "alive" zone.

The art was beautiful, the cocktails and *boquitas* (or "little bites") delicious, and the company outstanding. Dorothy introduced me to another expatriate, Mrs. Joan Paire Monati. Joan was an impeccably dressed, petite blonde ten to fifteen years older than me. We struck up a conversation, and I realized how much I missed having friends. It was so wonderful to be out and about and meeting people. In her youth, Joan had met and fallen in love with a Guatemalan lawyer of Italian descent. He was just home from a professional sojourn in Scotland, smoked a pipe, and had a bit of a Scottish burr in his English accent. He must have been dashing! Joan had accompanied a realtor friend to Guatemala, who was hoping to make this country a new tourist destination. It was kismet!

After a whirlwind courtship, Joan returned to Connecticut engaged. I learned all this later over many evenings and a few glasses of wine. But this night, she told me she had a room for rent and wondered if I was interested. I hated the tiny apartment the school-found for me. I didn't have a television or even a radio. Life was bleak—working all day and then home to this sparsely furnished and cramped enclosure. The next day I took a taxi to her house and almost burst into tears of joy.

Her home was a beautifully furnished little house with a magnificent garden and grounds. Joan had gone to a "finishing school" in New England, had impeccable manners, and a maid. Since she had been divorced from her dashing lawyer many years before, renting out a room allowed her to enjoy the lifestyle to which she had become accustomed. We bonded like two peas in a pod. I moved in and rejoiced at my good fortune. Things were looking up.

Really looking up. Angie called. Angie and I became friends in 1992 when I was teaching a special education class and she was the art teacher. While purchasing supplies in a craft store for a school project, the owner asked if she taught art. He then gave her a number to call. His friend booked itinerant lecturers for cruise lines, and they were looking for people to teach arts and crafts. And that momentous occasion was the beginning of our traveling around the world.

Our friendship grew several years later, when we both began teaching in a rural school district where we remained for over twenty years. Angie talked me through and supported me during my separation and divorce. Angie introduced me to cruising. We were lifelong close friends, and remain so today.

She wanted to come for a visit. I was ecstatic and excited. On my way to the airport to pick her up, I kept repeating Joan's address; "Veinte uno Avenida Vista Hermosa dos, Veinte uno Avenida, Vista Hermosa dos. After an enthusiastic reunion, we hailed a taxi, and I confidently repeated, Veinte uno Avenida, Vista Hermosa dos, por favor." "*Oh my word,*" Angie squealed, "you can speak Spanish already?"

"Yes, yes, I can. I can say, 'Veinte uno Avenida, Vista Hermosa dos, por favor.'" We still laugh about that. All these years and lessons later, my Spanish is still a mix of body language and charades with a noun thrown in now and then.

Angie and I had a wonderful few days together. She toured the school and the campus and was very impressed with the beautiful brick buildings, the Olympic-size pool, the new library, and the manicured grounds full of blooming tropical flowers. We shopped at the central market, went to several incredible museums, traveled to Antigua on a chicken bus, and visited the lively village of Jocotenango. *Tenango* means the "place of," so this town was named for the joco (*hoe co*) fruit grown there. This was the first of several vacations Joan, Angie, and new friend Maureen and I would share through the years.

Angie went home and reported to all our friends and peers that maybe I wasn't crazy after all. Many of them thought I was running away from reality, or maybe I was depressed. Angie cleared all that up, thankfully. I proceeded to initiate the innovative ideas I had to enhance the educational program and morale at the American School of Guatemala's lower school.

# Attending the Symphony

I was so happy living at Joan's and valued her friendship more and more as the days went by. I also appreciated and enjoyed Dorothy's company. She was very talented and was performing at the national theater with a visiting conductor, David Rouch, from Johnstown, Pennsylvania, and the National Symphony Orchestra. Joan and I accepted Dorothy's invitation to attend. Set on a hill overlooking Guatemala City, the theater was an architectural wonder of parabolic swirls and vaulted cement. The private boxes descended from the ceiling, clinging to the modern, multistoried structure like old spaceships coming back to earth.

The opening performance of the season was Dorothy. This beautiful blonde swept onto the stage, dazzling in a full-length red sequin gown, and took her place at the grand piano. Her expertise was enviable and her interpretation of the music, flawless. The piano was submissive and her mastery magnificent. After a standing ovation, the visiting conductor was introduced.

The Guatemalan orchestra was formally dressed in white tie and tails, and the stage was set with an empty back row of chairs and music stands. David Rouch conducts with every fiber of his being. Even Rouch's synapses trembled with joy as he led the ample musicians out of mere mediocrity and into the dizzying heights of magnificence. Guatemalans were proud. Visitors were awed. The beautiful compositions flowed without flaw. The performance progressed without incident on through the program. However, for those of us with inquiring minds, and a little tenure here, the empty back row remained a mystery.

Finally, in the middle of the 1812 overture, a row of uniformed men resplendent with braid and buttons solemnly took their places in the back row. With no introduction or fanfare, they simply began to play—picking up in the middle of the movement. Suddenly, one of these musician/officers left his chair, dropped out of sight behind the stage. And just before the climactic crescendo of the reprise, set off a detonation that rocked the house. After several seconds of stunned silence while the audience collectively checked their body parts, our attention became riveted on the stage, drawn by some primal, macabre instinct—waiting for whole sections to fall off their chairs. Instruments shattered and broken, victims of an unstable government. But everyone went on playing. Nothing happened. The conductor was reaching a new zenith of ecstasy as this famous 1812 Overture music filled the senses.

Then, it dawned on us that this was, indeed, part of the performance. Now this may be creative art in the first world, but down here, right now, in the middle of a civil war, bombs, or any facsimile thereof, in public buildings are somehow…unnerving. As sensibility was returning, the officer on the floor with the firecrackers really got warmed up. Detonation after detonation reverberated through that acoustically perfect theater, until the audience rose to their feet in a spontaneous ovation of surrender. Nothing like it. Culture, classical music, and bone-chillling fear. Another night out in Guatemala. I loved it.

# A Starry, Starry Night

Every time I visited Antigua, I discovered something new, became more in awe of its antiquities. It is generally agreed that Antigua, Guatemala, is the most spectacular city in Guatemala, and indeed even a contender for one of the most spectacular cities in the world. Its architecture and artifacts belie the fact that it is in the New World. Antigua is truly a piece of Spain suspended in time. Situated in the central highlands, Antigua is known for its preserved Spanish Baroque-influenced architecture. Many of the churches, cathedrals, and monasteries were damaged in the eighteenth-century earthquakes, but most are repaired enough to be used.

After living in Guatemala City for over a year with my wonderful friend, Joan, I was longing for some autonomy. I relied on public transportation, taxis, and Joan to move around the city and the country. I didn't want a car, but I did want some independence. Antigua is about twenty-four miles from the city, and there was a private school bus service to the American School. Shops and stores were within walking distance. Living in Antigua was the perfect solution for me. I began looking for a small apartment there.

I found just what I was looking for at the Hotel Ana. It was a gated facility. The apartment had a kitchen, bedroom/living room, and bath. What had been a swimming pool was now a grassy expanse just outside the back door. It was perfect. I reveled in being able to walk to a little grocery store, the market, the park, and many beautiful restaurants. The mercado was wonderful, and I shopped there almost every weekend. Fresh fruits and vegetables grown all over the country were on display and almost every flower—beautiful bunch after beautiful bunch. I could never resist their beauty, filling my little home away from home each week with vibrant color.

Parque Central has been described as the beating heart of Antigua. Centrally located, and just a block from my apartment, it boasted a magnificent fountain and many benches under beautiful jacaranda trees. It was small enough to be a perfect meeting place. "Meet me at the park" was a mantra for tourists and residents alike. My apartment was on the street of the famous Arco de Santa Catalina. The arch was built by the Spanish in 1690, and boasted a backdrop of the dormant volcano, Agua, making it a popular tourist spot and definitely presented a "Kodak moment."

I spent my weekends touring the ruins and sampling the coffee houses and restaurants. Joan came to visit often. One of our favorite restaurants was just across the street from Hotel Ana, and we loved to eat lunch there alfresco, with Joan's dog, Gigi napping at our feet. The menu was very eclectic and the gardens and dining room spectacular. The arched ceiling of the main dining room was brick. It was beautiful and a testimony to the value Antiguans put on esthetics. On my last visit, I was amazed at the expansion of this wonderful facility. A whole new wing of rooms had been added, including a beautiful pool artistically integrated into the interior of the complex.

This famous town hosted many cultural events, tour groups, weddings, and celebrations. Soon after I moved there, I attended the performance of the Guatemalan Modern and Folkloric Ballet enhanced by an exhibition by the Guatemalan Orchid Society. Using a huge variety of orchids as stage decorations was brilliant. Orchids and classical music and ethereal dancers—almost too much for mere mortals to digest. That afternoon was one of those indelibly imprinted in my psyche.

Several friends and I were sharing a coffee one afternoon and discussing our weekend plans. We all agreed that we should attend one of the open-air concerts by the Guatemalan orchestra on Saturday night. The San Jose El Viejo church ruins was a popular spot for such performances. The large courtyard hosted many outdoor events. We arrived early and were able to watch as the orchestra set up, tuned up, and prepared for the concert. The performance began as the sun went down. The music was flawless in the talented hands of those formally dressed musicians. The night was clear and black. As the moon rose over this august assemblage, every star in the universe vied for attention. The metamorphosis of the sky into a sea of diamonds was beyond description. A starry, starry night.

# Hotel Museo Casa Santa Domingo
# Restaurant and Resort

I loved living in Antigua with all it had to offer. My very favorite place, however, was the Hotel Museo Casa Santa Domingo Restaurant and Resort. It was actually an active archeological site, and the dig was ongoing. The monastery was founded by the Dominican Friars in 1542 and was the largest, richest monastery in Antigua. The earthquakes in the eighteenth century devastated the buildings, and they suffered pillaging for building materials through the years, so the property was in bad shape when it was purchased by a North American archaeologist in 1970. He carried on extensive excavations during his tenure. It is testimony to the vastness and opulence of the Santo Domingo that this ruin has been actively excavated since the 1970s, and the dig is still active well into the twenty-first century.

When I was living in this beautiful ancient city, the ruin consisted of several dining rooms, furnished with original artifacts, saints, statues, and ornate carvings. It was already a museum surrounding a restaurant, a hotel, a spa, theater, and a grand auditorium. Many special events were held in this unique venue. The center courtyard was used as a stage, and large black nets over the entire space provided shelter from the tropical sun.

On one occasion, Joan and several other friends and I attended a celebration in the grand auditorium. I had never been in that part of the Santo Domingo, so I didn't know what to expect. A crowd gathered outside in the center courtyard, waiting for the doors to open. What a surprise! We entered a wide hall with a gentle slope spiraling downhill. Hundreds of candles in niches lit the way round

Restoration under way at the Santo Domingo
Ruin in Antigua, Guatemala

and around ever downward into a very large subterranean room. The acoustics were perfect, the program entertaining, the venue outstanding.

By 2019, this complex was not only a hotel and a restaurant. It currently houses a jade factory and museum, an archaeological museum, a pottery and wax workshop, and a silver museum. All these in addition to the areas that were open in the early 1990s. So many reasons to love living in Antigua. Living there was like living in a kaleidoscope. Every turn brought another cathedral, another convent, another museum, another monastery, another spectacular ruin. I feel privileged to have lived there and to have had the opportunity to experience the living history of a city suspended in time.

# Welcoming New Staff Members

Instead of taking a year abroad prior to entering the workforce, some new graduates looked for alternatives that would support them while having a bit of adventure before surrendering to adulthood. Most of our new teachers were among the latter group. Some were certified teachers, some were not. Some spoke Spanish, most wanted to learn. And all of them had an adventurous spirit. I always began my welcome in-service by telling them we had much in common. They were seeking adventure at the beginning of their careers, and I was looking for adventure too, but I was doing it at the end of mine.

I knew they, like I, would be off on chicken buses every weekend, exploring the wonders of Guatemala and Central America. With the exuberance and naivete of youth, it concerned me that these fresh new faces would blunder into some difficult situations or be victims of opportunists and thieves. Cautioning them, lecturing them, was all well and good, but I quickly realized the need for some structured and supervised excursions. Another visiting administrator agreed that some off-campus orientation was a proactive approach. Initially, we even helped finance these excursions. Taking interested new faculty to educational research facilities, introducing them to ecological regions, and providing possibilities for volunteer work on their vacation time was beyond beneficial. These trips acclimated our visiting teachers to safe travel in this Third World country, highlighted some important cultural differences, set an example of respect for the Maya, and supported camaraderie among new hires. Taking teachers on field trips at first seemed strange, but the benefits soon became apparent.

The possibilities for destinations seemed endless. Guatemalan teachers volunteered to lead some excursions, and administrators contributed ideas. They even began to subsidize these excursions. We were able to integrate the continuing influx of staff each semester with minimal incidences. And I taught them to always expect the unexpected.

# Teacher Field Trips

Embracing my new job, I was conducting workshops, giving new teachers orientation assemblies, presenting seminars on whole language. At one of these seminars, I met Father Schaffer. He had been working in Guatemala for twenty-seven years and had an active *parroquia* in San Lucas Toliman. San Lucas Toliman is located on the southern shore of Lake Atitlan, one of Guatemala's leading tourist attractions. At an elevation of 5,400 feet, this spectacular crater lake is surrounded by the soaring volcanoes of San Pedro, Toliman, and Atitlan. *National Geographic* declared it to be the most beautiful lake in the world. Dug-out boats ply the pristine water connecting villages. The sounds of Cackchiquel, Tzuthuil, and Spanish blend as fishermen launch their dugouts and share fishing stories.

Father Schaffer invited a group of teachers to visit his parroquia. He generously offered housing, meals, and tours of his many and varied projects. He started an orphanage in this war-torn country. Fifty percent of the children housed there were victims of military conflict. He was also running a reforestation project, as well as an agricultural program, a nutrition program, and a housing project. His personal lifetime goal was to see that every indigenous family had a proper cookstove with a chimney.

My teachers were overwhelmed. They quickly volunteered to work during their holidays and semester breaks. Father was a wise man. He got many, many hours of volunteer work from energetic, young people who were reveling in being able to help these beautiful people. They brought back to their classrooms a new understanding of the culture and beauty that is Guatemala. This was a very successful excursion. In fact, the impact of these trips was so apparent that the American School administrators began to approve them. That was truly amazing, because this was not one of my most popular ideas, initially.

I was very grateful that the parroquia provided transportation for these young people in officially marked vans. This was a country still in the throes of a civil war, and guerillas were in and around Father Schaffer's area. Tour buses were occasionally stopped and people robbed at gunpoint. In fact, Joan came up close and personal with an attempted robbery. She and her constant companion, Gigi, were on their way to the town of Panajachel for the weekend. Gigi's little poodle eyes were fixed on the road ahead as she sat upright in the passenger seat. Just as they crested a hill, several guerillas with shotguns jumped out of the jungle and into the middle of the road at the bottom of the incline. Aghast, with chills up and down my spine, I haltingly asked what happened. "Well," this soft-spoken, demure, and cultured lady said, "I stepped on the gas and flew down that hill as fast as my little car would go."

"What happened to the men?" I asked in shock. Joan wasn't sure, but she did hear a thump as she sped past them! So you see, travel is always a bit of a risk. Expect the unexpected.

# Seeking the Elusive Quetzal Bird

Another one of the first tours I organized for the visiting teachers was to take a group of eager educators to a national park up in the highlands. We were looking for the quetzal (*ket sall*)—the national bird of Guatemala. It is a small bird, but has long, curved, emerald-green tail feathers. The Maya used those feathers in their ceremonial headdresses. One of my teachers in the English program had been in Guatemala a number of years and had married a Guatemalan. Robert had a van and very generously offered to lead an excursion to the *Biotopo*, or national Park, in the Altiplano (highlands). The cloud forests of the Altiplano are a haven for the sacred quetzal bird, the national symbol of the country. The long bright green feathers curve forward and symbolize the divine to the Maya.

Several of us were eager to go on another adventure. We left the city just as school was over on a Friday afternoon and arrived at a cottage arranged for by Robert, just before dark. The plan was to get into the park before sunrise Saturday morning in order to increase our chances of seeing the beautiful bird in its natural habitat.

Crude steps had been hacked into the dirt leading up the mountain. After about a half hour of hiking, I realized that we had not taken one single flat step. The trail led up, up, up. These cloud forests are very humid, almost to the point of being wet, so the trail was a bit dangerous. The mist was thick, and the sunrise splintered by the moisture in the air. The forest was pristine and beautiful. An enchanted place. Searching every treetop scanning the sky, listening, and watching for movement was intense. Try as we might, none of us even caught a glimpse of that exotic bird.

We set off for the city early Sunday morning, stopping along the way to marvel at the beautiful vistas and the breathtaking mountains. Roughly halfway to the city, Robert's van began to sputter and cough. Oh no! Nothing could be worse than breaking down in the highlands. Soon Robert pulled off the road and announced that his van was broken down, perhaps permanently, and that there were no tow trucks in the highlands. This was the early nineties. None of us had cell phones, and there were no towers, anyway, where we were. Just before total despair set in, a pickup truck full of men pulled over and offered help. It was wonderful that Robert was fluent in Spanish and could converse with them.

Now, when you are living and traveling in a country torn by civil war, where guerillas are still fighting the government and truckloads of armed militia turn up without warning, there are two things you do not want to do. Two things to avoid at all costs in Guatemala are getting in trouble with the police—there are horror stories galore about the prisons (we won't go there). And you don't want to get mixed up in politics. This was an election year, and the truck was full of men holding banners extolling the virtues of the candidate of their choice.

The truck looked like it was a model from the forties or fifties and probably had never seen a car wash. It was decided that they would tow us to the nearest service station. Our rescuers were very helpful and produced an ancient, short rope with which to pull the van. Trying to be chivalrous, Robert suggested the women ride in his vehicle, and the men climb into the open bed of the truck.

That is where I drew the line on this adventure. Our excursion just became a potentially life-threatening episode. There was no way I was going to be dragged up the next mountain, and the next and the next, at the end of that ragged rope. And what would happen on the way down the other side? I quickly jumped into the truck bed and happily took my place next to the sign that read, "Vote for Jorge Carpio." I'll never forget it. We were in the middle of a political campaign!

The other women joined me, and our poor brave men reluctantly had to get back in the van. The truck, careening around turns and struggling up inclines, was definitely overloaded. Fortunately, we had to make frequent stops as each man came to the footpath leading off the road to his village, making the load lighter with every stop. After no more than seven or eight men left the truck, we were pulled over by the police. As in most Third World countries, the police are corrupt, expect bribes, and have been known to treat foreigners with contempt.

First politics, and now the dreaded police.

The officers were telling Robert that towing a vehicle in these mountains was illegal, and carried a steep fine. And then the Spanish got too heated and fast to follow even for the most fluent among us. We huddled together, visions of rats and dark holes flashing through our heads. Frankly, I felt more helpless and victimized and terrified than I ever remember.

Suddenly, Robert produced his wallet, took out a card, and showed it to the officers. They scrutinized the card, handing it back and forth, and then the mood changed. Smiling and nodding, we were waved on our way. A miracle. What happened?

What we had assumed was a driver's license was, in fact, a medical insurance card from a local hospital—in English. The officers were not bilingual, which Robert had gambled on, and they recognized only the medical symbols.

"Doctor?"

"Si," Robert replied.

"No hay problema, Doctor. Disculpe. Adalante." (Sorry, go on.) We continued our death-defying parade through the dusk in a truck held together with paperclips and string, and the van illegally tethered a few feet behind. The trip ended at the first garage, where we all waited for the next chicken bus to take us into the city.

Our excursions were all turning into adventures, and now, some even dangerous.

# The Cascade Falls of Semuc Champey

At the American School of Guatemala, the five-acre campus encompassed the lower school, grades K–6, the upper school, grades seven to twelve, and the three levels of higher education at the University of the Valley, undergraduate, graduate, and doctoral programs. We had a closely knit staff at all the schools, and the administration was interconnected in many ways.

A professor at the university was organizing a trip to one of the natural wonders of the highlands (the Alta Verapaz). Located in the heart of the jungle, the Semuc Champey cascades are one of the popular tourist attractions in this area. Home to jaguars, tapirs, macaws, toucans, and many other beautiful animals, this was going to be an interesting trek through an exotic land. It would be a three-day, two-night trip. The bus would leave on Friday afternoon, traveling all night, with an arrival at the village of Lanquin early on Saturday morning. There was some hiking involved, but nothing strenuous, I was assured. It sounded exciting, and quite a few of my teachers and I signed up.

In order to keep the costs down on these excursions, there was a great need to fill the bus. Well, they not only filled the bus—they overfilled it. The original seats on this old school bus had been replaced by wider ones from a larger bus, in order to put three people on each seat. This left an aisle only wide enough for one leg. Ah, my first clue that there may be more details to this trip than were disclosed. We traveled through a dark and moonless night on unpaved, unmarked, mountainous, rough roads. Every fiber of our beings were in erratic, relentless motion for many miles. Sleep was impossible.

We made two stops, the first at a well-lit wayside tienda open for business awaiting our arrival. There we could buy soda, cookies, and candy. In Guatemala, when you buy a soda in the countryside, they pour it into a baggie and keep the bottle for recycling. I found out later the bare straws were washed before reusing them! Our last stop was to answer any calls of nature. After all the vibrating, this stop was well received. Men went to the front of the bus and the women to the back. I was traveling with a fifth-grade teacher from North Carolina and her eight year old daughter. We each had a backpack full of bare essentials.

We pulled into the small village of Lanquin, still wet with morning mist, and were greeted by a mariachi band! At five o'clock in the morning! This village was so high in the cloud forest that the villagers didn't even speak Spanish. Our bed rolls were taken into the community center where we were to sleep. There were no hostels, no hotels, no restaurants. We were in rural Guatemala. Gwen was fluent in Spanish, but it didn't look like that was going to help us here. We filed out of the bus and began the hike into the cascades. Ironically, there was a crude paved road, but one too precipitous for the vintage school bus. The road was wet from the morning mist and difficult to navigate. On the way uphill it was like clawing your way up a stone wall and then going down the other side caution was necessary to prevent sliding on the slippery surface. It was not a fun hike. After three or four hours of climbing and descending, I made up my mind that there was no way I was walking back out of there. I didn't know how I was going to avoid it, but I knew I wouldn't survive that rigorous trip twice in one day. By now everyone was way ahead of me. I was all alone, trudging along on my fifty-plus tired legs when, wonder of wonders, I heard a noise. I heard a motor.

A motor! Just then, a nice, new pickup truck came into view. The double cab was full of young people having a wonderful time, headed for a dip in the beautiful waters of Semuc Champey. I stood in the middle of the road, arms spread, and stopped the vehicle. Using body language and broken Spanish, I asked if *I* could ride in the bed to the falls. "Si, si, señora, no hay problema, no hay problema." I was ecstatic. But I didn't want my peers and teachers to see me "wimping out" as we passed them, so I lay down. There I was, a director of the American School sprawled out in the bed of a stranger's truck. Shameful.

Soon we came to the end of the road. A muddy, narrow path led to the falls. Now I had to walk again. In minutes, my new sneakers were covered with mud and my pant legs as well. I began to collect mud on my shoes, like cows do on their hooves. Heavy layers of mud were clinging to my sneakers like clods, making walking even more difficult. When we finally arrived at the cascades, I was exhausted. Literally. The falls at Semuc Champey were beautiful. It was an enchanted soft green place in the middle of the jungle. But for me, it was not worth the torture to get there.

I sat on a rock, trying to recuperate, when Gwen and her daughter, Emily, came over to comfort me. Just as I was beginning to breathe normally again, we heard more people coming. Three men, in their thirties and forties, were approaching the water. "Gwen, you see those men? I'm leaving with them." They were so robust and happy that I was certain they didn't walk in. I was going to follow them out and hope for the best. Gwen was very concerned and begged me to reconsider. We watched as they took a dip in the beautiful green pool at the bottom of the cascades and proceeded to leave. I fell in step behind them, and soon Gwen and Emily followed. Sure enough, at the end of this suddenly beautiful trail, there was the most beautiful jeep I had ever seen. As we approached, these wonderful, kind men offered us a ride and then a beer. It was the most delicious beer I ever tasted. I was almost delirious at our good fortune! My prayers had been answered. I may survive after all. As I came back to reality, we learned that the men were supervisors at a sugar mill and were exploring Guatemala on their Saturday off. We were very lucky. And so ended my visit to the famous cascades at Semuc Champey.

After thanking them profusely, they dropped us off at the school bus. The driver remained on the bus, waiting for Sunday morning to drive us back to the city. I walked all the way to the back of the bus (one leg at a time), and opened my backpack. I had wisely chosen a packet of "handy wipes," black silk pajama bottoms (because they rolled into a tiny, light ball), a black T-shirt with *Greece* in bold gold letters across the front, a pair of flip-flops, fresh underwear, a paisley scarf, and a grapefruit. I got out of my mud-encrusted jeans and sneakers, used the handy wipes, and changed clothes. I was a sight to behold with my eclectic, color-coordinated, clean and dry, strange new outfit. I had planned to wear the jeans for the entire trip and use the pajamas at night, but it turned out that I needed them long before bedtime.

Gwen and Emily were involved in cleaning up also, and we decided we were not sleeping on the floor of the community building with no supper. Somehow Gwen was able to learn about a little hotel about a mile out of town with a restaurant nearby. Just as we were leaving, the first few people in our group came straggling into town. They were soaked, having been caught in a cloud burst; they were cold and they were hungry.

We walked to the hotel, paid for a room, and then walked to the restaurant where we enjoyed a hot meal of chicken, black beans, and rice. Sunday morning, we boarded the bus and headed down the mountains toward Guatemala City. But the professor had one more delightful surprise for us. We stopped to explore an undeveloped cave. I decided not to take the tour. I didn't like the sound of "undeveloped" in the context of "cave." Gwen and Emily described it as awful. The path through the cavern was covered in guano from the millions of bats who lived there for decades. The path was slippery, the only light was from their flashlights, and there were no banisters, which made for slippery slopes. I waited on a rock at the mouth of the cave and watched the bats fly in and out.

I survived another adventure in this wild and rugged country, but this time my survival was almost a miracle, literally. Another lesson in expecting the unexpected!

# Visiting the Rio Dulce

A few weeks after Angie's first visit to Guatemala, I got a call from Maureen. She wanted to visit. I was thrilled, and we decided on dates and times, etc. A few weeks later, the parents of one of our second graders, also expats, invited me to spend a weekend with them at their second home on the Rio Dulce River. The Rio Dulce, or sweet river, flows into a large basin forming Lake Izabal. Robin and Steve had been in Guatemala for over a decade. They built their dream getaway on a bluff overlooking the river that flows from Lake Izabal out to the Caribbean. It is a safe harbor and popular wintering spot for sailboats and yachts from all over the world. They owned their own plane and hired a pilot to take them back and forth until Steve was to get his pilot's license. It sounded wonderful, and I really wanted to go. But Maureen was due to arrive that week. Robin assured me that the house was big, and another guest would be a welcome addition.

"How would you like to spend a weekend on the Caribbean coast of Guatemala?" I asked Maureen in our next phone call. She assured me that the weekend trip sounded great and a flight in a six-seat Cessna would not be a problem. The following Friday, our hostess picked us up at school in her SUV. We collected her daughter, Madeline, and joined the rest of the crowd in the vehicle. We were traveling with a Rottweiler, a full-sized poodle, and a macaw. The large, beautiful bird was returning from the coast after a visit to his veterinarian in the city.

Maureen said she knew she was in for an adventure when we were asked to help roll the plane out of the hangar. Robin's husband, Steve, got in the front with our pilot, Louis. Maureen and I were in the middle seats, and Robin and little Madeline were in the back. The animals were wherever they wanted to be. The macaw was loose in the plane and free to fly from shoulder to shoulder, nibbling on buttons and earrings and leaving little "terms of endearment" on our backs. The flight was a short forty-five minutes and the scenery spectacular, soaring over rugged mountain peaks and volcanoes. However, suddenly, the downdrafts that day were worse than this little family had ever experienced. After the third or fourth alarming punch earthward, Maureen stopped talking, her face became terribly white, and her fists were tightly clenched.

Louis fought to control the heavily loaded plane as we bounced our way toward the coast. Now, when I get nervous, I tend to chatter. When I sense someone else is nervous, I chatter even more. So I pleasantly began to point out coffee plantations, large farms, orchards, hoping to distract my clearly distressed friend. Nothing worked. Maureen literally had white knuckles, was staring straight ahead, and was completely unresponsive. Just when I thought this flight couldn't get any worse, Louis announced we were going down. Those words hung in the air. "Look over there!" he shouted. The sky was purple and churning. "We can't fly through that storm. We have to land somewhere!" the pilot insisted. By now we were over Lake Izabal. Louis found a small airstrip carved out of the jungle and started his descent. "Don't you *dare* land *there*!" Robin shouted from the back of the plane. "That's a Nicaraguan drug-runnin' strip," she drawled in her Alabama accent.

Suddenly, Maureen's head began to turn until I was in full view. "She's not kidding, is she?" my terrified friend managed to ask in a lifeless tone. With that, we were on the ground under a purple-black sky and coming to a stop just as the turbulence of the storm hit. Fighting to walk against the wind, we discovered a two-story small cinder block building with huge vats inside. So Robin was right. This *was* a drug-running strip. Now even more terrified than when we were in the air, Maureen led the charge back to the plane, as Louis was screaming for us to get on board. The storm had quickly passed, the sky was clear and blue once again, and Louis wanted to get out of there. He taxied to the end of the short runway, heading to the lake, and called on all the power this little plane had to take off. Even our eyelashes were vibrating as he revved the engine to its full capacity. When he finally started the takeoff, it was do or die. Thank heavens it was successful, because as we climbed over the trees, we saw six men on horseback, holding rifles and accompanied by dogs, racing toward us and the airstrip.

We were only minutes from the house, and Louis circled the beautiful grounds twice, signaling the caretaker to come for us by boat. Louis headed back to Guatemala City, and we proceeded to Robin and Steve's waterfront getaway. Their thatched-roof retreat was magnificent. It was huge and square and full of custom-made, hand-carved furniture. There were porches on all sides with French doors allowing the house to open completely to the outside. White pea-cocks gracefully strolled the manicured grounds, and the views were panoramic. After that tumultuous start, the weekend went smoothly with leisure time to enjoy the beauty of the lake and river. We char-tered a boat to take us to Livingston, a town on the Caribbean coast where we enjoyed an alfresco lunch of freshly caught local fish. We enjoyed a swim in a hot spring and returned to the house in time for dinner. Robin and Steve were exceptional hosts, and the dinner that night and breakfast on Sunday were spectacular. We flew back to the city without incident.

Joan and I joined these friends for the weekend several times after Maureen's visit. Picking us up one Sunday afternoon for the return trip to the city, one of Louis's landings on that little airstrip was quite precipitous. The nose of the plane dug into the soft earth, and he was unable to free it. I was late getting to school Monday morning until we were able to hitch a ride with a friend and neighbor who luckily had some empty seats in their plane. Louis, Robin, and Steve stayed behind getting their Cessna ready to fly again.

# Adventures with Family

My family is quite adventurous. We all seem to have been bitten by the travel bug. Through the years, we have enjoyed many family trips. We like each other's company and travel well together. And that is not always the case. In all my life adventures, there were a few times that my travel companion was not pleasurable. Only a few, thankfully. Traveling is a kind of like a litmus test. It sorts people out rather quickly. My niece, Misho, was graduating from college and I offered to take her on a cruise to celebrate. We had a wonderful time plying the Mediterranean Sea, experiencing all its spectacular beauty, teaching arts and crafts, of course! We both loved to dance, and we were regulars at the disco every night. One night, we had a particularly good time getting down and dirty with several Welsh couples. They were witty and charming, and we not only danced the night away, but laughed it away as well. In fact, we stayed in the disco until it closed. The next morning, we got up with barely enough time to get to our ten o'clock class. After class we were walking out on the deck when I felt something sliding down the leg of my slacks. There at my feet were my pantyhose from the night before. Talk about jumping into your clothes! And then there was the tour to a monastery in Greece we almost missed. After the tour we stopped at a little cafe and enjoyed grape leaves and a beer. Stuffed grape leaves still take me back to that unusual breakfast.

What a wonderful way to get to know the young woman that Misho had become. Our itinerary was wonderful. Athens, Mykonos, Santorini, Lesbos, and then Venice. We stayed a few days in Venice and visited all the usual tourist spots. Our hotel was right on the Grand Canal. From Venice, we flew to Heathrow and met my sister-in-law, Ruth (Misho's Mom) and her daughter-in-law, Heather. We rented a car and dear, patient Ruth drove us all over the British Isles. Brother Jim and Ruth had lived in England right after they got married. Their first child, John, was born there. So Ruth was the designated driver since she had become used to driving on the left during those years. We met our Vance relatives, looked for Nessie in Loch Lomond, and shopped everywhere. We had a wonderful time.

Soon after our British Isle trip, I ran into Father Schaffer. I was telling him about my family coming to Guatemala and asked if they could bring anything for his many projects. When I met them at the airport, I couldn't believe the luggage those dear girls were carrying. Ruth went to local laundries and dry cleaners and ask for any diaper "culls." What an ingenious idea! Then she hit hardware stores and markets for seed packets. Misho and Karen got discarded Spanish books from high schools. They had huge ski bags filled to the brim. Father Schaffer called me to confirm the dates and informed me that he would send a van to pick us up at Joan's house. I had planned to rent a car. As grateful as I was, I had planned to travel to Chichicastenango after visiting his parroquia. No problem. His van would take us wherever we wanted to go!

We stayed for several days at the parroquia in a beautiful cottage originally designed to house nuns. We each had separate bedrooms and were invited to dine at the priest's table each night. It was an incredible few days. Our chauffeur and tour guide took us to many of Father Schaffer's projects. We stopped at homes in the remote villages where there were babies. Young mothers were so grateful for the diapers that they brought their babies out for us to admire. This was very unusual in the Mayan culture. The men of the villages were thankful for the seeds, and we deposited the books at several schools.

But it was the orphanage and infirmary that knocked our socks off. So many beautiful children, victims of a war-torn country. Parents would walk for days to get their sick child to Father's facility, hoping to save their lives. Ruth is one of the most compassionate people I have ever known. She has been seen crying at airports when she witnessed strangers tearfully bidding their loved ones farewell. She is a soft and sweet and compassionate person. These facilities were too much for her. Having orphaned children cling to you crying, "Mamma, Mamma" is enough to break down the strongest among us. These two places were almost too much to handle. We have so many exceptional memories the normal tourist never has an opportunity to experience. I have thanked Father Schaffer over and over for making my family's trip so memorable. Up to this point, it was the trip of a lifetime. Our African safari would come in second, several years later.

We toured Antigua, visited the ruins, went to several museums, enjoyed wonderful meals at five-star restaurants, and shopped the local markets. But I saved Tikal for last. I wanted to experience this ruin of an ancient Mayan city for the first time with my family.

# Tikal

Tikal is an archaeological site in the middle of the Tikal National Forest. It was the ceremonial center of the Mayan world during the Classical Period. It is the largest and most impressive Mayan ruin in Guatemala. The towering pyramids in the Central Plaza are 186 feet and 212 feet, making them the highest structures in the western hemisphere at that time. In 1979 Tikal was named a UNESCO World Heritage site. The national park is a rain forest and home to beautiful and exotic animals like toucans, macaws, coatimundi, and the howler monkey.

From the moment I knew my family was coming to visit me, I began to plan. I wasn't content to just take them to the usual tourist sites. I wanted to give them an overview of this whole rugged, intriguing country. I began to refine the itinerary so that we did museums and cultural tours, contrasted by taking them back in time and immersing them in the Mayan world. I wanted to contrast the modern with the ancient. Considering that I didn't have a car, this became quite a challenge. But I saved Tikal for last. I wanted to see this ruin for the first time with them.

Getting to Tikal isn't easy. It is an hour flight from Guatemala City to Flores, the closest town in the northern section of Guatemala. Then, it is an hour bus trip to the national park. We arrived in time for lunch then set off with our guide through the jungle. How seventeenth-century people built such sophisticated temples and pyramids is beyond belief. A walk through that park is almost indescribable. Climbing those architectural wonders is an experience of a lifetime. We heard toucans, macaws and saw a coatimundi (Central American version of a raccoon). Near the end of the tour I asked about howler monkeys. "Oh, you want to see howler monkeys?" our guide said. "Well, if we're lucky, I know a good spot, and they may be still taking their afternoon siesta." Off we went to a heavily forested area with large, mature trees. There they were! Movement in the top branches caught our eyes, and we could not believe our good fortune. The whole family was there. Papa was dozing on a stout branch, Mama was higher up in the canopy, supervising, while two babies were practicing acrobatics. We were mesmerized. They leaped, hung, swung, and twirled.

The howler monkey is the largest of the New World monkey species. Their fur is long and generally black, but some variations in species do occur. They have a distinctive call that is low and gutteral increasing in volume up to a very high-pitched loud grunt. It's like saying *oh, ooh, oooh*, as low and loud as possible. We watched until siesta was over, Papa woke up and took off, with the family following. We were truly blessed to see this wild animal up so close in its native habitat doing what howler monkeys do.

In the early nineties, The Jungle Lodge was the closest hotel to the park. Their electricity was provided by generators and turned on for only a few hours in the morning and a few in the evening. Our lodging was quite primitive. After this full day, when we finally got to our room, I flopped down on the nearest bed. My daughter started to yell for Ruth and Misho to come quick. "She's lying down! She's lay-ing down!" Karen yelled. I didn't realize how my ambitious itinerary was impacting my visitors. They were as exhausted as I was!

At dusk, we heard a few howlers calling in the park. But dawn was a different matter. Because we were in a national park, I was shocked to hear the roar of heavy equipment, almost to the point of shaking the earth. At dawn, when the first howler calls, he is joined by a magnificent chorus of the entire population, loud enough to literally shake the jungle. Our "bulldozers" were actually howlers greeting the dawn! The howler monkey's call can be heard from two to three miles away even through dense rain forest. To add a colorful closing note to our Tikal experience, the tree just outside our room was full of macaws. Vibrant red, blue, yellow feathers in profusion with a background chorus of howling. Wow! Tantalizing Tikal.

# Looking for Property in Belize

My brother is an entrepreneur. He is one of those people who always land on their feet. He has had many ventures over the years, some of them wild, but nearly all successful. His longest tenure and most lucrative employment has been as an auctioneer. Small house and estate auctions led him eventually to auto auctions. One of his weekly jobs is at an upscale auto auction in Fairfield, New Jersey, very close to New York City. After mentioning in casual conversation that his sister was in Guatemala, one of the guys started to tell him about property in the Caribbean, specifically Belize.

Jim liked the idea of owning an escape from the cold and snowy winters in Pennsylvania. I imagine visions of palm trees, pineapple frappes, hammocks, blue skies, and frothy waves danced in his head. I got a call at school from this charismatic man I'm proud to call my brother. The excitement in his voice was infectious. He wanted me to go to Belize and look for property for him. Whoa! What an assignment.

My friend Maureen was still in Guatemala and she agreed to go with me. We were just finalizing our plans when Maureen got a call that one of her investment properties was on fire. Unfortunately, that left me alone on this fact-finding mission, which I knew from the start would be an adventure. I was just hoping it would be an adventure and not a disaster. Jim assured me that a friend of a friend of a friend would meet me at the airport in Belize City and escort me to several properties on the mainland and then to the island of Cay Caulker. He suddenly turned stern and serious. "Now, listen to me, Carol, *do not bring home any packages*. Do you understand? Do not bring home any packages."

I was too shocked to speak. Back in the day, as I approached womanhood, it was my father who talked to me about the birds and the bees. It was my father who monitored my dates and curfews. It was my father who repeatedly intoned, "Don't bring home any packages." (Our code words for remaining pure!) A package meant a pregnancy. So I was thoroughly confused when, thirty some years later, my own brother was telling me the same thing. After I could speak again, I shouted into the phone, "Oh for heaven's sake, Jimmy, don't be ridiculous—I'm fifty-two years old!"

At this point, I think Jim was having second thoughts about asking me to go to Belize. He began to worry that I would be going alone, and then someone at work evidently cautioned him about the drug traffic so prevalent in the islands. His cryptic message, literally was "Don't try to bring or smuggle home any sort of package as a favor to anyone." I didn't get it until much later. Jimmy didn't know about Dad's admonitions; he's nine years younger than I. I was incredibly naive about drug trafficking, so it became one of Jim's favorite stories about his sister. And he has many. Storytelling is one of his talents, and he can reduce the most staid among us into helpless convulsions of laughter. Sometimes at my expense.

Since I was traveling alone, I tried to look professional and business-like. I carried a briefcase and a camera, and put on my most serious demeanor. The flight from Guatemala City to Belize City was short and the airport crowded. I had no idea who was picking me up, so I waited and watched as people met their visitors and loved ones. After everyone had reunited, there were only two men remaining. One was way over six feet tall, wore little circular sunglasses, and pants that looked like they belonged to Sinbad the Sailor. The other was shorter than I and had equally bizarre clothing. My heart fell as they approached me. Oh no! Jimmy, as much as I love you, I'm going to inflict bodily harm to your person as soon as I see you again. If I ever see you again! Thus began the downward spiral of this adventure.

The situation kept deteriorating as they led me to an El Camino. An El Camino, with one bench seat in the front. I reluctantly got in, because I didn't know what else to do. They conversed among themselves in Garifuna, a dialect with the lilt and rhythm of the tropics that I was trying desperately to understand. *Wait until I get my hands on my brother; wait until I get my hands on my brother*, kept echoing through my head like a mantra. But I had to concentrate on what was happening. We wove our way through the crowded streets of Belize City and quickly broke into the open countryside.

They took me to several properties that were on the market. I took pictures and made notes, hiding my trepidation behind a brisk and serious exterior. We returned to the city and boarded a launch bound for Cay Caulker. The launch was operated by a macho young man who avoided the trough of the waves at all cost by accelerating to a point bordering lunacy. We sped across the water, hitting only the white crests of the waves. It is extremely difficult to maintain one's dignity on a vessel at full throttle going hell-bent for leather. Wait until I get my hands on you, Jimmy. Just you wait.

It was a short walk from the water taxi dock to the Sunshine Hotel. Everyone knew this tall fellow, J. J., and people came out of their houses to greet him. Now I was getting some of the words being spoken, and to my chagrin, heard one elderly woman say, "Ah, you like the old chickens now, eh?" Yikes! My dander went up, and all my caution lights went on. I didn't like this one bit. We stopped to meet an American who was to take over showing me properties. This retired auctioneer looked like he stepped right out of Margaritaville. Over dinner, and after several rounds of tequila kicked in, John revealed that J. J. was a star basketball hero and had led the Belize team to glory. A celebrity of sorts. Pieces of the puzzle were beginning to fit together.

Speaking of celebrities, Cay Caulker is one of Bob Marley's favorite haunts, and he owns a home there. After making arrangements for the next day, they escorted me to the hotel. The Marin family has owned this quaint resort for decades. They are clean, honest, friendly people and I relaxed for the first time since this odyssey began. In 1991, the only way to get to the island was by boat. There was no air service and very few hotels and restaurants. That is not the case today, but back then, The Rainbow Hotel was like my little secret.

I met my daughter and her husband there the following year, and we had a wonderful time, snorkeling, taking boat tours, exploring the island, and eating stone crabs. I arrived a day ahead of them because there were only two flights a week out of Guatemala to Belize City. Tom and Karen followed my instructions and found their way to the water taxi in the center of Belize city. On the launch to Cay Caulker, Mrs. Marin greeted them and asked where they were staying. "I don't know! My mother is there and will meet us at the dock," Karen explained.

"Oh," Mrs. Marin said, "is your mother always laughing and smiling?"

"Yes, yes, she is," Karen said.

"You stay with us! You mamma waiting for you!" the Marins announced.

Over the years, I returned to the hotel several times. Their children had taken over, remodeled, expanded and built a restaurant in front of the hotel out on the water. It remains one of my favorite destinations.

The island is small and news travels fast. After my obligations to Sinbad and Mr. Margaritaville were complete, and I had prepared a report for Jimmy, I had a few days to enjoy myself. However, I felt quite vulnerable being alone, in spite of the Marins's friendly "adoption" of me. At that time I was still a member of Outdoor Writers of Pennsylvania and Outdoor Writers of America, and I made It known that I was writing an article about fishing and tourism on the island. I felt this would give me some credibility and respect should anyone get any ideas about me.

Belize, the small country on the east side of Guatemala was formerly British Honduras. It has the largest barrier reef in the Western Hemisphere and is the second largest barrier reef in the world, spanning 180 miles of coastline. I was ecstatic. So much to do, so much to see. Ernesto Marin recommended a glass bottom boat tour in lieu of snorkeling, which I had not mastered at that time. And he arranged for a fishing trip out near the reef. After the boat tour and a bite to eat, I eagerly jumped into a fishing boat with Russell, a friend of the Marins as my guide. In spite of dusk approaching, I didn't want to stop fishing. The bottom of the boat was covered with fish, enough to feed the island, I suspect. When we finally pulled up to the hotel dock, Ernesto was waiting for us. He was worried about me, and chastised Russell for keeping me out so long!

In another aside, after I flew back to Guatemala and Karen and Tom were still enjoying their tropical vacation on Cay Caulker, Russell took them out for a night snorkel over the reef. Flashes of lightening illuminated the coral for seconds at a time, and the luminescent organisms put on quite a show. Seeing bioluminescence is one of nature's most ambitious theatricals. They enjoyed a wonderful time in Belize.

My last day on Cay Caulker was poignant. I wasn't ready to go back to reality. After another death-defying trip in the water taxi, I needed a place to stay before my flight back to Guatemala in the morning. The Marins had recommended a bed and breakfast in Belize City. The house was a beautiful example of majestic Caribbean architecture and the hostess delightful. Her father had been a judge in Belize City, and she had grown up in the house. Miss Isabal was delightful, outgoing, and full of stories. She graciously invited me to dine with her. We had the best fish-head soup I've ever tasted. I was so thankful for a perfect last day and a perfect last night in the country of Belize. But best of all, I was slowly forgiving my brother for getting me tangled up in this latest chapter of life on the edge.

I had a little balcony off my room with a view of the main street in Belize City. I will never forget the Sunday morning parade of well-dressed worshippers, especially the woman, dressed in every vibrant color of the rainbow, walking to church in their beautiful hats and carrying their umbrellas as a shield against the intense southern sun. It was like a painting come to life.

On the plane back to Guatemala, watching the dense jungle slide under me, I had time to reflect back on those last few days. I was savoring the memories, the boat ride, the fishing, the beautiful people I met, and I could feel myself unwinding. In retrospect, it was a wonderful interlude, despite the rocky start. Maybe I'll spare my brother any violent acts. In fact, maybe I should thank him for a wonderful experience. And so ended my first visit to beautiful Belize.

# A Week in Lyme Cay

One of my Guatemalan teachers had become a good friend. She had a lovely family, and I often traveled with them to relatives in the highlands near Coban. Carmen's husband was an architect, and his office was arranging a trip to an island off the east coast of Guatemala. Again, in an attempt to fill the bus, Carmen was inviting teachers along. This time I ask a lot more questions. The bus was a Greyhound, the island undeveloped, and the snorkeling supposedly fantastic.

We would leave Puerto Barrios at high tide, which was roughly 4:00 a.m. There would be a service crew who would set up the tents and provide three meals a day. It sounded wonderful, and the cost was incredible: 125 dollars per person, which included bus transportation to and from the boat, the boat, tents, and meals. The boat would stay with us for the week and provide excursions to other islands in the archipelago. It sounded wonderful, and quite a few of us signed up.

Undeveloped. I imagined we would go to bed at sunset, and arise at dawn. I imagined the food would be condensed or dried, along with some fresh local fish. I imagined I would get bored with snorkeling. So I brought some good books, candles, as well as the suggested flashlight, matches, and a few sticks of beef jerky, just in case.

We left Guatemala City a little later than planned, because two students were trying to get a wave runner in the "basement" or luggage compartment in the bottom of the bus. Only when they had exhausted every possible angle and removed as many things from the machine as they could did they finally give up and we set out for the coast.

This was my first hint that some of my vacation companions had a wild streak. I began to question the sanity of some of their antics. Where were they going to put the wave runner? Surely not on the boat? Or did they intend to tow it for six hours on the open sea? Or worse yet, ride it? And then I saw the first bottle of Johnny Walker Red. Oh boy! Here we go on another adventure. Sleep was not even an option, as the party got louder, and the contents of the bottles kept diminishing. We traveled through the night, down out of the mountains and into the coastal town of Puerto Barrios

We arrived at the dock about 4:00 a.m. and there, waiting for us, was an old wooden boat that looked like a Chinese junk. A cook-stove dominated the center of the deck, and a roaring wood fire was browning freshly made tortillas. A big pot of black beans bubbled slowly, and there was enough rice to feed us for a week.

The captain was in his fifties, round and jovial. He looked like there must have been some pirates in his family tree. The crew was busy settling us all in, stowing the luggage in the hold, feeding us, and watching the tide. We had to wait almost an hour until the tide was high enough to allow us to pass out of the bay and into open water. Soon we were out on the open sea. I sat in the bow, my legs dangling over the side to catch some warm Gulf Stream waves. That was one of the best parts of the trip for me. I will never forget moving through the black velvet tropical night watching the stars and constellations of the southern sky. The big dipper was not scooping up—it was pouring out! That fascinated me.

I especially loved it when the water got rough. As we climbed each wave, and descended into the trough, watching the next swell coming, it was like being on an amusement park ride. The warm water of the Gulf Stream got me wet, and sometimes even crashed onto the deck. I was awake all night, not wanting to miss a minute of this glorious journey.

Just as the night was spectacular, the sunrise was breathtaking. The trip took us five hours. The island was small. There was no dock. All our supplies, food, luggage, had to be carried to the beach. We climbed down the ladder and walked or swam the one hundred feet or so to the shore. Lyme Cay was an island paradise.

The crew—there were eight or ten of them—set up camp in no time. Tents were erected, a fire built, the food organized, and then... wonder of wonders, I saw big, big speakers being connected, tropical lights strung, and a generator cranked up.

The books never got read, the candles were never lit, the jerky went untouched. We snorkeled every morning. Two or three steps into the calm water, and the beauty of the sea was indescribable. The fish were prolific and the corals amazing. One of the architects kept a boat on both coasts, and he generously offered to take anyone interested out fishing. So every afternoon, I walked into the water and climbed the ladder to his beautiful, sleek fishing boat. The fishing was wonderful, and the cooks enthusiastically prepared our catches. We dined on delicacies from the sea. The conch ceviche was unsurpassed, the spiny lobsters huge and succulent.

Several afternoons, the captain would take us on his yacht to explore other islands, gather shells, swim, and sunbathe. Our nightly DJ had an eclectic mix of music, but his collection was dominated by Bob Marley. Bob vacationed frequently on nearby Cay Caulker and was a local celebrity. And that's how I learned to reggae—barefoot in the sand, under the Caribbean stars. The quintessential wife and mother now totally morphed into a free, independent warrior, marching through life with joy and wonder.

The week flew by. Time stood still. Sunsets were a quiet time. Several of us would gather on accommodating rocks right on the shore and drink in the wonder of it all. The rest of the world was light-years away. This was truly a magical vacation.

# Meeting a Mayan Saint

My hostess and dear friend, Joan, is one of the most curious and inquisitive people I have ever met. She is intensely interested in all things in her environment. She has traveled most of the world, studied watercolor in the Japanese style, collected information on the many species of palm trees indigenous to Guatemala, and has an active fascination with Guatemala and the Mayan culture—to just scratch the surface of her curiosity. She has taught us the art of interviewing people, and you can find some very interesting people in Guatemala. I venture to say, I didn't meet one dull soul while I was there.

So Joan is constantly gathering information and loves to share. Maureen, Joan, and I were spending several days in Panajachel, before heading to the Pacific coast for another few days. After a lovely lunch overlooking Lake Atitlan, and talking with a few other tourists, she excitedly announced that we could visit the Maximon. She pronounced it *mosh e mahn*. The who? It seems that this pagan Mayan deity "sleeps around," and although his permanent home is in Santiago, Atitlan, every Holy Week he travels to a new home and is difficult to find. Joan has always wanted to see him, and she just found out where he was. Did we want to go? It was obvious that she did!

Well, tell us more about this Mayan God, Joan. Maximon is a wooden idol dressed like the Maya themselves and an indigenous representation of San Simon. However, it seems that this old boy has a bad reputation. His notoriously hedonistic urges were uncontrollable, so the villagers cut off his limbs, making him rather short and squatty. He lived an unbridled lifestyle and was always seen in his signature black hat, with a cigarette in his mouth. Worshippers brought

Worshiping the ancient Mayan Deity, the Moshimon

him offerings of cigars, cigarettes, and spirits, which he supposedly imbibed in to excess. How interesting and macabre! A friend told me the Maximon was mentioned in Indiana Jones movies. Evidently, he transcends cultures.

And so it was that we set off for the village that was being visited by Maximon. He was in a church, and worshippers were lined up outside, waiting to get in. The church was in the Spanish style, whitewashed on the outside with many statues of saints and biblical figures in niches on the inside. The churchyard was full of little smoky mounds of burning copal, or incense. The solemn line of people moved slowly, and I realized with a start that we were the only gringos there. As we moved into the church, letters extolling the virtues of various parishioners, nominating them for sainthood, covered the walls. The church was dimly lit and the air heavy with incense. As our eyes adjusted to the light, we realized that after each worshipper had made it to the front of the church, they had to wait to be escorted to the center by a man in full Mayan attire. Standing behind Maximon was a woman with large, dark, and incredibly crossed eyes. She wore a red bandanna and carried a broom of grasses. While loudly intoning ancient chords, she soundly "whipped" each visitor until they made their offering and turned to exit, hopefully, cleansed of their sins. The Maximon stared stoically ahead with eyes that were dead. A very solemn and haunting aura hung in the air.

I was just beginning to become uncomfortable and think that we should get out of there, when after the third or fourth beating, I almost jumped out of my skin as a trio of men, dressed as Spaniards, appeared out of the smoke and broke into very, very loud music and song. Wow! We were amazed, excited, titillated, and downright scared. Hoping Joan wasn't going to join the procession to visit Maximon and get a beating, Maureen and I had to leave.

We were bursting with emotion. Should we cry or should we laugh? It wasn't until we were all safely in the car and on our way back to Panajachel that we exploded with hysterical laughter. What an experience. Meeting a Mayan saint was definitely more excitement than we had bargained for. This time, we did expect the unexpected.

# Becoming a Patron of the Arts

My birthday was coming up, and Joan wanted to do something exciting to celebrate. Many villages in Guatemala have a specialty. One may be the village of weavers, another the village of pottery, and so on. Joan decided we should go to San Juan Comalapa, the village of artists, because she knew how much I admired the primitive art that decorated stores, shops, restaurants, and her house.

A man named Andreas Curruchiche (1891–1969) was the first brave soul to put down his hoe and take up a paintbrush. In an agrarian society, this was a very bold move. Instead of raising food to feed his family, he decided to pursue his talent and earn a living from his artwork. It was a shocking gamble and probably not one well received by his family.

Because of Andreas's incredible talent, he became famous internationally and San Juan, Comalapa, became known as the Florence of America. He delighted in teaching his techniques with oil paint, and many of his students, grandchildren, and great grandchildren are still painting today. The Curruchiche (*coo row chich a*) name is famous in Guatemala. Today there are over five hundred artists living in Comalapa and painting in the Curruchiche style.

The village of Comalapa is home to the largest mural in Guatemala, depicting scenes from the pre-Columbian period, through colonization, earthquakes, the Guatemalan Civil War, to the present. I was very excited to be visiting this unique village and looked forward to our little trip with great excitement. What a wonderful birthday present! Comalapa is not far outside Guatemala City in the department of Chimaltenango, or area of the chimneys. As you drive through the town of Chimaltenango, you pass acres of red bricks drying in the sun.

Just past the village is the turn off to Comalapa. The center square was ringed with little tiendas selling Kaqchikel (*cot chi kel*) paintings. I wanted to meet and see the works of a Curruchiche, and so we were given directions to David Curruchiche's home and gallery. It was like stumbling into a diamond mine! Much of the art was done in the primitive style, but there were several oil paintings done in the traditional genre. I chose a rather large, three-by-four scene of a cobblestone street in Antigua, with walls covered in bougainvillea and brilliant white Spanish domes in the background. It was a beautifully done landscape of museum quality, I thought. It hangs in my living room today and brings back vivid memories of that birthday present. I also bought several primitives depicting church holidays and festivals.

We were most happy to meet David, and Joan introduced me as a director of the American School. I conveyed through Joan how honored I was to meet him. And that, we thought, was that.

Two weeks later, David showed up one morning at the American School with several helpers, all laden down with paintings! He was escorted to my office. I was astounded. Now, how should I handle this, I thought, trying to remain calm. Would the administration become upset? Was I on the brink of a reprimand? Then I realized that I really didn't have control of the situation, as the men began to unwrap David's artwork. My office had turned into an art gallery.

Throwing caution to the wind, I sent out a memo to all teachers, inviting them to my office during their lunch period or after classes. The turnout was phenomenal, and the paintings disappeared. It was very gratifying to see these proud men in their best clothes, complete with cowboy boots and impressive cowboy hats, beaming from ear to ear at their good fortune. David was ecstatic.

And so I became a patron of the arts. David came to the school once a month from then on, with an ever-increasing inventory of work. Visiting professors, university professors, upper school staff, and even administrators attended my popular "art shows."

My Stoltz oil painting of a street in Antigua

# Vacationing in Retalhuleu

Retalhuleu is in the southwest corner of Guatemala known as the Pacific Lowlands. It stretches from the mountains of the east to the Pacific coast. It is a three- to four-hour drive west from Guatemala City and, at a lower altitude, enjoys a tropical climate. It is hot and it is humid. The area produces sugarcane, coffee, cotton, cacao, and rubber. Early in her marriage, my hostess, Joan, lived in the nearby city of Mazatenango for a while when her husband was practicing law there. She knew about a small resort outside Retalhuleu that had become a popular, economical vacation destination. Gwen, Emily, and I were ready for a completely relaxing respite from the academic world. Joan made all the necessary arrangements, and during our Easter break we set off in Joan's car for some fun in the sun.

The rooms were crude wooden structures up on stilts. They were clean, but had no glass in the windows, no air-conditioning. By now we were accustomed to Third World surprises, and we settled in without incident. The resort was lovely and very tropical. The pool was large and well maintained, the kitchen served excellent ceviche—what more could we ask for?

The design of the rooms seemed a little strange, and so we began to ask some questions. It seems the United States Central Intelligence Agency built this camp/resort to train Cuban defectors and American troops for an invasion of Cuba. The CIA? An invasion? We were fascinated. This location was chosen for its proximity to the climate in Cuba and soldiers trained here in 1960. The USCIA gathered, funded, armed, and trained this anti-Castro rebel organization. Known as the Invasion of the Bay of Pigs, it was a closely guarded piece of intelligence until April 17,1961, when these troops from Retalhuleu, known as Brigade 2506, stormed the beach of a small bay on the south coast of Cuba. They were ill prepared, ill equipped, and lacked military support. Their defeat was an embarrassment to John F. Kennedy's first term. The Bay of Pigs went down in the annals of our country's history. Three women and a little girl had no idea when we laid our heads on a pillow that night what tales those primitive walls of our room could tell.

The week went quickly, and we enjoyed the laid-back pace of this Pacific paradise. We swam, played games, talked, and got to know each other better. The only exciting thing that happened on this trip was a thunderstorm that blew up suddenly. We were all sitting at the pool relaxing when the sky began to churn with ominous-looking clouds. We weren't ready to leave the pool and took a rather nonchalant attitude to the impending storm. Suddenly, a bolt of lightning the size and width of a telephone pole punctured the earth fifty yards from where we were sitting. That did it. We scrambled for shelter and thanked our lucky stars we were not any closer. The next day we found, on the ground, a charred circle that was at least three feet in diameter. Somehow, someway, even the most tranquil of excursions in this country turn into an adventure.

# Celebrating a Quince Años

When a girl reaches her sixteenth birthday, in our culture, that is a milestone to be celebrated. Daughters are often given a "Sweet Sixteen" birthday party. In the Latino culture, they celebrate the fifteenth birthday. Carmen and her family were going to Coban to the Quince Años of her niece, and they invited me to go with them. I appreciated these invitations so much, because with them, I wasn't a tourist any longer. I was a friend of the family and included in special times like this one.

Santo Domingo de Coban is the capital of the Alta Verapaz. At an altitude of 1320 kilometers, the area is lush and laden with orchids, including the rare monja blanca, or white orchid. Coban is 219 kilometers from Guatemala City and is one of Guatemala's major coffee-growing areas. The population is Mayan and Q'eqchi (*key shay*). It is one of my favorite destinations, but this visit was very special. It was a wonderful weekend, full of festivities and music. No stone was left unturned for this party.

The family owned a hotel, so there was plenty of room to house all the visitors and relatives. Early Saturday morning, we were serenaded at our doors by a trio of mariachi musicians. What a way to be awakened! It just got better and more over the top as the day unfolded. The entire hotel, courtyard, and gardens were humming with activity. A florist had been brought in from the city, with a multitude of tropical flowers, each more beautiful and vibrant than can be described. She was in a work space outside the hotel, making outrageous floral arrangements for the church, the dining room, the gardens, and patios. The Mayan culture revels in the cacophony of colors that cover their landscape, and they weave those colors into their clothing, linens, gardens, and their lives.

A banquet was being prepared, tables set up in the large dining room, and soon the kitchen was producing wonderful aromas. There were helpers and service people everywhere. It was a perfect time for me to stay out of everyone's way and enjoy some alone time in the garden. As I sat under the tropical sun, bathed in warmth and wonder, this whole tableau unfolded before me. It was like I was in a dream, and I didn't want to wake up. How did little Carol Vance, the butcher's daughter, end up in this mysterious and mythical land?

All too soon it was time for the festivities to begin, and everyone assembled to start the parade to El Calvario Church. The church was a spectacular example of Spanish architecture. White arches laden with crimson bougainvillea vines invaded the senses as stately columns guarded the niches displaying ancient saints. Built on top of a hill, this facade commanded the highland valley. Thin wisps of mist lingered in the late morning sun with the mountains in the background, making a magnificent backdrop. As we entered this sacred place, a hush fell over the celebrants as we absorbed the beauty of the interior and the pews, laden with white calla lilies. I was awed. I was honored to have been included in this magical chapter of a young woman's life.

By our standards, this birthday bash was opulent. Carmen's niece wore a white ball gown for the church service. This symbol of purity accentuated the patina of her skin. Her gleaming black hair was caught in an elegant coif, transforming this young woman into the epitome of a Spanish beauty. Amazingly enough, she appeared at the banquet in yet another incredible gown, and then donned a third garment for the music and dancing that followed the meal. I reveled in the contrasts of cultures.

# At the Beach

Annelisse, one of our Spanish teachers, was married to a Guatemalan doctor who was serving in the military. He was from Quetzaltenango (*ket zall tea nango*) meaning "Place of the quetzal" up in the highlands. This area was also known for vibrant handblown blue glass and the highland produce. His family still lived there, and to defray costs of the trip to visit them, he and Annelisse would often invite visiting teachers along. They were a lovely family of four. Joe was handsome, and Annelisse was very petite and very beautiful. Their little girls were two and four years old, and both looked like their mom and Shirley Temple.

The Guatemalan government provided cottages on the Pacific coast for the officer's rest and relaxation. Annellisse and Joe would often invite teachers to also stay there with them. Another teacher and I were looking forward to this particular trip. The weather was wonderful, the forecast bright for the weekend. I can still see those gorgeous little girls with their curly, curly hair bouncing up and down on their mother's lap with anticipation. They loved the beach.

I always sort of "catered" these excursions. I'd bring along cheeses, dips, and snacks in addition to an easy-to-heat-up meal. The cottages were three bedrooms, right on the ocean, and immaculately clean. We all enjoyed the ocean and the sun and the sand all day Saturday. The weather was glorious as predicted. Sunday morning, I made a large breakfast, and we all took off over the volcanic black sand to dip our toes in the water. The waves were too rough for swimming, but the ocean breezes were refreshing, and the children loved playing in the sand.

We all enjoyed a light lunch and packed to go back to the city while the girls took their naps. It was late afternoon when Annelisse announced that her husband had a headache and was lying down. By then, the sky had become cloudy, and the wind was picking up. Finally, Joe got up, loaded the car, and we set off. By now it was pitch-black and had started to rain. The trip back was several hours full of anxiety, as Joe struggled to see the road and stay on it in an almost blinding rainstorm.

The other teacher was dropped off first, then Joe drove me to Joan's house. Just blocks after her house, Joe suddenly drove up on a sidewalk. He told a terrified Annelisse that he couldn't see. If not cared for properly, the produce in Quetzaltenango can harbor an organism of some sort. It travels to the brain and becomes a pupa. When the worm emerges, it emits a burst of protein into the brain, which was what caused Joe's terrible headache. I know it sounds like science fiction, but this worm heads straight to the optic nerve and begins to nibble it away. Luckily, they got to the hospital in time. However, they had to send to the United States for the medication that would kill the worm before Joe lost his sight completely. He recovered and finished his term in the service. We were very, very lucky that Joe didn't lose his sight on the long trip back from the beach in that awful rainstorm.

Years later, the Bucks County Organization for Intercultural Advancement Board was visiting our school in the sugarcane area, near the Pacific coast. As usual on our annual visits, we brought educational materials and several professors from universities to present seminars and conduct teacher workshops. During a short break, I walked into the teacher's room and there, having lunch, was Annelisse! We couldn't believe it. She was no longer a teacher and was at the southern campus of the American School as a textbook consultant. It was great fun catching up. She and Joe had divorced, she remarried, and the girls were now young women. Proudly presented photographs depicted what looked like 3 beautiful sisters. All three were incredibly beautiful women. It was wonderful seeing her again.

# Chichicastenango

Santo Tomas, Chichicastenango, is a village in the highlands of Guatemala perched on the crest of a mountaintop at 2,193 kilometers, way over 11,000 feet. Getting there is an adventure unto itself. Riding in a bus unable to maneuver the hairpin turns is unnerving. Driving the 140 kilometers northwest of Guatemala City is not for the faint of heart. Driving a straight-shift vehicle is downright suicidal. Joan's little car was a straight shift, and I was driving.

Chichi, as it's called, is in the El Quiche (*key shay*) Department and home of the K'iche' Mayan culture. The town is named for the four-hundred-year-old church that was built atop a pre-Columbian temple platform. There are twenty-one Mayan languages, and K'iche' is the prevalent language there. It is about two to three hours from Guatemala City and boasts the largest outdoor market in Central America. The market is open on Thursdays and Sundays and features every conceivable product made or grown in this creative little country.

The road to the summit is a convoluted series of hairpin turns too tight for a long vehicle, so tour buses routinely cross the middle line and leave smaller vehicles like cars or SUVs no choice but to stop and let them through. In a straight-shift car, this becomes a nightmare of clutch shifting, starting, and braking. We somehow navigated these hazards and arrived in due time at the market. Joan, Maureen, and I were spending a magnificent Sunday in the highlands shopping. It was a beautiful day, and we enjoyed a bountiful lunch in the dining room of the Santo Tomas Hotel. A huge fountain dominated the courtyard, and women were busy at their backstrap looms, weaving the famous textiles. Macaws roosted throughout the dining room, and an accomplished marimba band provided Latin music. An idyllic setting. An afternoon to write home about.

And then disaster struck. Joan's car wouldn't start. It was too late in the day, and on a Sunday no less, to do anything. It was the height of the tourist season, and the hotels in Chichi were very crowded. We decided to get on a chicken bus and go to Panajachel for the night. We'd solve the car problem on Monday morning. The buses were getting crowded as shoppers left the market and headed back to their villages. There were few single seats available when we boarded, so we separated to find seats. I had bought a *cofridia* drum used in religious ceremonies and held it on my lap like a shield. Joan, Maureen, and several other English-speaking passengers were seated several rows behind me. The last indigenous passenger to board the bus was visibly intoxicated. Weaving and struggling for balance, he made his way down the aisle to my seat where he passed out in a heap on my lap.

Tossing my drum to Joan, I literally levitated up out of my seat and turned to face the back of the bus. Passengers began to click coins on the side of the bus—a signal of trouble for the attendant, and people were shouting, "Are you all right?"

"No!" I screamed and, with that, proceeded to make my way to Joan's seat, striding over frightened little Mayan people, who were certain they were going to be crushed by the robust American gringo. To this day, I have no idea how I got out from under that man, out of that seat, and over those frightened people.

To get to Panajachel from Chichicastenango, you have to change buses at the crossroads of Esquintla. By the time we got there it was dark. Really dark. There were crowds of people waiting for transportation. A young man was nice enough to offer us a ride in his truck bed, for a fee. An enterprising fellow. He assured us he was going to Panajachel. Rather than wait for a bus, we joined a half dozen or so people already sitting in the truck bed. The road to Solola is narrow and winding. A difficult drive in good conditions, in the daylight. Navigating that treacherous road in the dark takes skill and nerves of steel. Riding in the back of an open truck gave this stretch of road a whole new dimension and one we were not anxious to repeat. We got to Solola, a village halfway to Panajachel, and the truck stopped. Joan's Spanish was really coming in handy on this night that seemed like an endless nightmare. This is it. This is as far as he goes, Joan reported. Now we're back to waiting for a bus.

Chicken bus is not just a colorful or cute name for the buses in Guatemala. It is a very descriptive name. Chickens do ride the bus. Sometimes they are in a crate tied to the roof, and sometimes they ride in someone's arms along with the other passengers. Frequently, avocados, mangoes, coffee, and even pigs ride on the roof. Riding a chicken bus is almost always an adventure. On popular routes, people are packed so tight on the seats and in the aisle that the attendant can barely make his way through the crowds to collect fares. If the bus passes a police checkpoint, the driver yells "Get down" in Spanish, and all the people in the aisle drop to their knees and bow their heads so the bus won't get pulled over and charged with overcrowding.

I've been on a bus with no windshield wipers. To compensate for this, the attendant walked to the back of the bus carrying a bucket of water. He opened the back door, swung onto a ladder, climbed up to the roof and walked on the roof to the front of the bus. This brave young man threw the bucket of water over the windshield to clear it, all while the bus was traveling at maximum speed climbing the steep side of a volcanic mountain, or hurtling down the other side, buses are poorly maintained, and there are no vehicle inspections.

Standing at a bus stop in the dark, waiting for one of these conveyances was bad enough, but then it started to rain. The road from Solola to Panajachel on Lake Atitlan is all downhill. Hairpin turn after hairpin turn on a rain-slick, black, narrow road produced an adrenaline rush equal to a ride on a roller coaster. Somehow, we made it in one piece. We vowed never to leave Chichi in the late afternoon, even if we had a reliable car.

Monday dawned bright and beautiful. Joan phoned her home in Guatemala City. Her maid's husband was staying in the city for a few days, and Joan told him where the spare keys to the car were. She arranged for him to take a bus to Chichi, get the car fixed, and drive it to Panajachel to pick us up! Life is so much easier when one has servants!

The idea of spending another day at Lake Atitlan was a wonderful way to end what started out to be a disastrous trip home. Lake Atitlan (*ah teet lawn*) is one of Guatemala's biggest tourist attractions. It is actually the crater of a huge extinct volcano and Central America's deepest lake. It has been lauded as the most beautiful lake in the world and is ringed by dormant volcanoes.

In Guatemala, each indigenous village had a distinctive style of clothing. The women's blouses, or *quipils* (wee peels) are especially distinctive and beautifully embroidered. They range from elaborate flowers to simulated needlepoint. I recently purchased a tote bag made from a worn quipil that I found in an upscale catalog! It is very distinctive. In Panajachel, the men's trousers are white hand-loomed fabric with a vertical black stripe every two or three inches. Many women embellished these knee-length pants by embroidering birds, animals, or other designs around the bottom of each trouser leg for their husbands. Quipils and trouser pieces and parts are sometimes offered for sale, if you are lucky enough to find them. At a market in Panajachel, I found a most unusual piece. It was the leg of a trouser with forty-two colorful, intricate, detailed, embroidered glyphs that a talented woman had copied from drawings found on a cave wall at the base of one of the dormant volcanoes. I purchased it the moment I saw it. It remains one of my most treasured mementos of Guatemala.

Over lunch in one of Panajachel's quaint cafes, Joan overheard people at the next table talking about Monterrico. They had just returned from several days at Johnny's Hotel, where we were going next. It seems there had been some robberies there at knifepoint. This was enough to trigger Joan's investigative talents, and she began to interview them. They assured her that the situation was under control. Johnny had hired an armed guard to patrol the hotel grounds at night. Johnny had patrol duty during the day. So another adventure was brewing! Mari's husband found us and chauffeured us back to the city. It was with some trepidation that we prepared for our trip to Monterrico.

# Canal de Chiquimulilla and Monterrico

The Chiquimulilla Canal runs parallel to the Pacific Ocean from the El Salvador border to Puerto San Jose on Guatemala's southern border. The road to the canal on the Pacific coast was narrow and unmarked. The first time I went there, I was driving Joan's car, and we were zipping along at a reasonable clip, when suddenly I saw a pig in the road. I immediately slowed down, and that was a good move, because without warning the road ended at the Chiquimulilla Lagoon. The village on the edge of the water was very small and the people very friendly. Joan paid a boy to "guard" the car, and we set off for Johnny's Hotel on the next barge. The canal was cut through marsh and wetlands and was alive with exotic flora and fauna. The mangrove wetlands along the canal are home to beautiful water lilies, water birds, even tropical America's semiaquatic caiman, a member of the alligator family. We were fortunate enough to see little four-eyed fish indigenous to this area, scurrying away from our primitive craft. A corrugated tin roof for shelter from the sun and crude benches were the only amenities. Around the first turn, another craft was approaching us. This vessel was a wood platform on some kind of buoyant floats and had two cows tethered to it. A man was deftly guiding it down the canal. The canal was an important waterway connecting towns on this side of the coast and had a lot of commercial traffic.

The air was heavy and still and the heat oppressive. Joan had booked us into the only hotel on the beach in a two-bedroom villa with a private pool. That private pool was going to be a lifesaver because the hotel was not air-conditioned. We were stoked for another adventure. The conversations in Panajachel the night before were fresh in our minds. Knifing and robbery here in this laid-back barely developed paradise? Seemed unlikely, but then we remembered that armed guards had been employed. We'll be fine. And then, suddenly, the sky was pink. First, bright sky blue and then covered with pink. I couldn't imagine what was happening. "Oh, that's a flock of flamingos," Joan explained. Maureen and I had to catch our breath. A flock of flamingos large enough to turn the sky pink—a sight indelibly seared into our memories forever. The unexpected!

Joan assured us that someone would meet us and drive us to the hotel. So far it sounded like a First World vacation. Two bedrooms, kitchen, private pool, oceanfront. We were getting excited. The barge pulled into the landing, and we proceeded up the dock. Waiting for us at the end was a tall, very muscled, tan young man extremely scantily dressed. A red bandanna held his blond curls, and the tiniest bikini we had ever seen, struggled to hold the rest of him. Sure enough, it was Johnny.

We put Joan in the cab of his old truck and Maureen, and I stood in the back as Johnny careened around turns and spun the tires on the sandy road to avoid getting mired down. Bushes and reeds slapped us in the face, and low-hanging branches could have done some damage if we weren't paying attention. Thankfully, we pulled up at the hotel still in one piece. Johnny drove us to our villa. Our villa. Our two-bedroom villa with a private pool.

The pool was the size of a child's wading pool, and it was empty. In broken German, Johnny assured us it would be full in no time. He hauled out a fire hose, turned some valves, and the Pacific Ocean began to pour into our private swimming pool. The front room was screened in and furnished with a table and four chairs. There was a sink at one end. However, the sink was not connected to anything and dripping water drained onto the floor. The bedrooms were small and had one window each, no glass. We were several steps beyond shocked. And we were several degrees beyond hot.

Shamelessly, we three lowered ourselves into just inches of cool Pacific water and began to relax as our body temperatures returned to hot-normal. We decided to make the best of it. We were here now. We could survive two nights, couldn't we? And let's not forget that an armed guard would be protecting us through the night. That's a plus, right? Maybe we wouldn't even lock the screen door… Lock the screen door—the only thing between us and things that go bump in the night? Really? Why bother?

As dusk approached, we were anxiously awaiting the arrival of the guard. Out in the courtyard, Maureen noticed a kid sitting on a rock. A young man of maybe thirteen or fourteen. Sure enough, he had a rifle across his lap. This was almost too much. What had been amusing, what had been disappointing, what had been disconcerting, was now outrageous. We were not happy campers! The sound of the mighty Pacific waves thundered and crashed ashore just beyond our "villa." Night brought a welcome drop in temperature and an increase in the ocean breeze. Joan and I shared the bedroom with two single beds, and Maureen was in the other. As difficult as it was to get to sleep, I finally did drift off only to be awakened by something crawling on my arm. I swiped it away, and it didn't go anywhere! Not wanting to wake my friends, I swiped again, more forcefully. I heard a soft thud on the wall behind my bed and quickly pulled the sheet tightly around my entire body, shuddering at the possible identity of my night visitor. My best guess was a tarantula! Or maybe it was a scorpion!

Morning dawned bright and beautiful. The hard-boiled eggs Mari had packed for us were welcome and wonderful. However, our ice was almost melted and the chest almost empty. It was a not a difficult decision to call Johnny and say goodbye to his "adventure hotel."

I returned to Monterrico many times after that with my friend and Guatemalan archeologist, Irma. She had a thatched-roof home there with a pergola out on the dune. We spent many wonderful star-kissed nights waiting for the moon to rise in the southern sky and watching the luminescent crests of the waves roll ashore. It was a wildly wonderful undeveloped corner of this charming country, and one that I grew to love.

The footnote to this experience is that in preparation to writing about Johnny's, I looked it up on the Internet. Believe it or not, twenty years later, Johnny's Hotel is still in operation, still called Johnny's. Only now, there are over one hundred rooms, a restaurant and bar, several large pools, and a new owner.

# To Carol

You do not need a mansion grand and tall.
On a scale of one to ten,
You have it all,
Health—that's wealth indeed. Glamor, talent, charm, and wit
Feel not chagrined,
You have neither failed nor lost
But gained and found yourself.

—Jenet Watters Vance 1987

# Adventures on
# the High Seas

# Bermuda

Having been on over seventy-five cruises as the arts-and-crafts lady, I have lots of cruise stories to tell. Because I lived close to several ports, I often got calls at the last minute to jump on a ship. My craft bag was always packed and ready, and I was eager to go. I enjoyed every single exotic itinerary offered to me, but also accepted trips that were repeats. Bermuda out of New York City was a frequent destination. Naturally, those trips had several noteworthy anecdotes. So I'll start telling you my cruise experiences by beginning with trips to Bermuda.

In 1511, Spanish Navigator Fernandez de Oviedo sailed close to the archipelago we know as Bermuda. He attributed the discovery of the islands to Juan Bermudez, possibly as early as 1503. A century later, the shipwreck of the Virginia Company's *Sea Venture* marked the beginning of a permanent settlement. News of the wreck inspired William Shakespeare's *The Tempest* in 1611 to 1612. Now there's a little-known fact and a great trivia question. Bermuda is in the western North Atlantic and is comprised of seven main islands and about 170 additional islets and rocks. It is about 650 miles east of Cape Hatteras, North Carolina. The archipelago is twenty-four miles long and less than a mile wide. The main island is about fourteen miles long and only a mile wide. The capital is Hamilton, and the islands are home to birds, lizards, and frogs. Not much wildlife!

Made famous by the Bermuda Triangle, or Devil's Triangle, this is the area of Atlantic Ocean from Florida to Bermuda to Puerto and back to Florida. Within these approximate boundaries there have occurred enough unexplained wrecks, disappearances, and suspicious activities to keep the legend alive. The jury is still out as to whether these mysteries have been substantiated. Bermuda is an internally self-governed British overseas territory with a parliamentary government. The British monarch is head of state represented by the governor. Bermuda was a frequent destination when I started to cruise.

## Rough Seas

An early April trip to Bermuda out of New York City sounded like just what the doctor ordered for two winter-weary northeasterners. Visions of crystal-blue waters, pink sand, and balmy beaches preoccupied our minds as we packed for this spring escape. Historically, the entire entertainment staff is introduced before showtime on the first night at sea. As we left the shelter of the Hudson River and entered the open sea, the weather began to deteriorate. By dinner the ocean was white capped as far as we could see. By showtime it was downright angry, and we estimated the swells at seventeen feet. Waves were crashing on the theater windows, which was mid-deck, mid-ship. The dance floor was made with stainless-steel tiles, the better for ballroom dancers to glide gracefully, but not good for navigating in bad weather. As the entertainment staff took to this treacherous stage, I wondered how I could remain upright on my fashionable high heeled shoes, much less look confident and composed. I managed to introduce the Arts and Crafts program and get back to my seat without falling. But it was a tumultuous night. Several dance routines were cancelled, the comedian was thrown out of bed and got a nasty cut above his eye. Anything not tied down in our cabin was on the floor. Because of the storm the ship was diverted further out to sea rather than sail past the Outer Banks. Three days in Bermuda flew by, and the return trip was smooth.

## A Bus Trip to the Beach

The approach to Hamilton is dramatic. The ship sails between two grand rock formations so close that from a distance it looks like you could reach out and touch the rocks as the ship glides through.

We docked right on the main street in Hamilton. You could window shop from our porthole! Not willing to risk life and limb on one of the famous Bermuda scooters, we chose a public bus ride to the nearest beach. My friend Pat and I were dressed like Frick and Frack in different-colored, but matching, strapless sundresses. This summer day was clear and beautiful. In anticipation of a lack of amenities at the beach, we were wearing our bathing suits under our dresses. We easily slipped out of those dresses and frolicked in the warm waters of the Atlantic Ocean. Now, to navigate the return to the ship raised several dilemmas. One, we were hot again; two, we were sandy; and three, we were wet. The only thing I could think of to do was to don those infamous dresses again, wriggle out of our bathing suits using the full skirted dress as a tent, as it were, and hand carry our swim attire back in our beach bags. Yes, Pat and I did ride a public bus in Bermuda sans proper undergarments.

## Learning to Snorkel

Several months later, Maureen and I were docked in St. George's and wanted to go snorkeling. So many places I traveled had fantastic snorkeling opportunities, and I was eager to learn. Every time my ears slid underwater, I became claustrophobic. I was determined to overcome this while we were in St. George's. Discussing this with a crew member, she suggested a perfect spot. A small, enclosed lagoon provided safety, security, and privacy as I sputtered, spattered, and splashed my way to success with Maureen's help. We returned to the ship wet, salty, exhausted, and looking like drowned rats, but I had learned to snorkel.

## Karen and Me and Bermuda

I wanted to give my daughter and her fiancé, Tom, a honeymoon for their wedding present. Now operating as a single parent, on a school teacher's salary, I had very little discretionary money. I came up with the idea of setting them up for a teaching cruise. My daughter was a certified teacher and a competent crafter. But just to guarantee that things went smoothly and eliminate any anxieties, I decided she and I should take a cruise together several months before the wedding. This was Karen's first cruise, and she was looking forward to it. I was looking forward to lots of quality time with my daughter. We had great fun designing our projects and gathering the required materials. I knew she would enjoy Bermuda and all it had to offer. Our first port of call was St. George's. The ship anchored just before lunch, and a large double-deck boat was waiting to take passengers ashore.

While we waited for the ship to clear immigration, we decided to have lunch in the dining room. As we approached the double doors, we were greeted by a very good-looking Bermudian. He was still sitting outside the dining room when we came out. Now he struck up a conversation. "Are you ladies going ashore?" he asked politely. When we indicated that we were, he introduced himself as the captain of the waiting boat. "I would be honored if you would join me in the wheelhouse for the trip over to St. George's." We readily accepted. He met us at the gangway and personally escorted us to the upper deck, to the chagrin of several passengers who saw this play out. The trip was smooth and the view incredible from the vantage point of the captain's deck. We munched on the peanuts he passed out, laughed, and told stories on the trip to shore. A grand way to start our visit to Bermuda.

## The Necessities of Travel

Later that day in St. George's, the ship's horn blew several times, calling all passengers back to the ship. Karen and I had a cabin on a short lateral hallway, with another cabin directly opposite. In New York, as we watched fellow passengers embark the ship prior to sailing, we were impressed as a stretch limousine pulled up next to the ship. Two girls got out sipping champagne. Wow—these chicks know how to travel, we thought! Turns out they were in the room across the hall from ours. Our hall mates were nurses from Boston, and this was their first cruise, their first big vacation, and they were determined to do it up right. I think every piece of clothing Sue and

Sarah packed for this trip still had price tags on them. Their outfits were cutting-edge couture and very colorful.

But back to the ship's horn. Everyone hurried to get up the gangway, energized by their day in St. George's. Everyone but Sarah. After several louder blasts, the ship hoisted the anchor, and we were off to Hamilton. After a slow, leisurely voyage we docked in Hamilton the next morning. Karen and I were out on the deck early to watch the approach through the stone cliffs. I loved watching the docking process. Those big vessels just glided into berths and docks like they were cruising through butterscotch syrup, tying up without so much as a bump. It always amazed me.

A lone figure stood on the dock at the gangway. A lone bedraggled, sand-encrusted figure with matted hair and badly burned skin. She was shouting, "*Soda! Soda!*" Someone threw her a can, and she caught it eagerly. Oh my gosh, it was Sarah. A very tired, dehydrated, hungover Sarah. A case in point to always carry with you, when traveling, the necessities required for proper daily living.

## Mind Your Own Business

On another cruise to Bermuda, we were seated with some people from Alabama. We loved their Southern drawl and quaint expressions. One night, Angie and I were in the disco and an officer ask me to dance. I love to dance, so I accepted, of course. He was a good dancer, and we took several turns around the floor. The next evening, the Alabama couple opened the conversation with, "We saw you in the disco last night. We saw you dancin' with that officer," in an accusatory whine.

"Really?" I replied, sweetly.

"Yes, yes we did. But you wasn't doin' nothing wrong now, was ya?"

I could feel my blood pressure rising. I could feel my face getting red. I don't anger easily, but this was an affront beyond belief. Slowly, I turned to face this person with the back of my hand on my forehead and in my best and slowest drawl replied, "Whah I don't think so. *I never got one single complaaaaaint!*" Angie stopped eating. The table was drowning in silence. I calmly picked up my fork and continued my dinner. That was the last inappropriate word we heard out of those people.

## Will You Marry Me?

My Aunt Peg, Uncle Bud's wife, is an amazing woman. Uncle Bud died in his mid-sixties, and Peggy, as her friends called her, never had any inclination to find another partner. Bud was her one true love. This amazing lady was a master at Bridge, still went to a gym to work out through her eighties, read voraciously, and was extremely well informed. I loved her very much. She was peppy and fun. I invited her to be my guest on several trips and cruises. On one occasion, we sailed out of New York City on the *Queen Elizabeth II* bound for Bermuda. We were both excited to sail on this elegant, famous ship. It was very British. There were beautiful, formal fresh flower arrangements in all the public rooms, a "first class" library and a library for the rest of us, and a "first class" dining room. White gloved waiters served tea every afternoon at four. Many of the people who came on these cruises as my helpers were often by my side during the entire cruise. Where I went, they went. Not Aunt Peg. She went to all the Bridge games, attended mass every day, and often picked different excursions.

Therefore, on this particular trip, I was often off doing my own thing as well. I loved being at sea. I would often sit outside reading the afternoon away, or curl up in a corner of one of the lounges, reading. About halfway through the cruise, I began to notice a single man walking the ship. He was barely five feet tall and almost that dimension around. His estimated age was early sixties. One afternoon on his rounds, he spotted me sitting alone in one of the lounges. He stopped to talk. He was a friendly fellow, and I enjoyed our conversation. This was a perfect opportunity to "interview" him as Joan had taught me. I learned he was from Australia, never married, lived with his mother, and owned a very large sheep farm. He was cruising around the world.

Here is a lonely man, I thought. One evening, several days later, he approached me after the entertainment. Aunt Peg had gone to bed, and I was reading in the lounge so I didn't disturb her. Again, Mr. Australia began to talk about his life on the sheep farm, his interests, and hobbies. And then he dropped the bomb. "Would you consider becoming my wife and living in Australia?" I was speechless. Was he demented? How do you respond to such a bizarre request? His manner was very serious. This wasn't a joke. Trying hard to keep my wits about me and think of something to say, it seemed like time was suspended. I babbled something sweet and kind—I can't remember what I said, but I was careful to avoid him at all costs for the rest of the cruise. Boy, you really do meet all kinds of people. He was cruising around the world looking for a bride. Amazing. A marriage proposal! Now that was unexpected.

# Naples, Gibraltar, the Canary Islands, Portugal, and Morocco

My sister-in-law, Ruth, and I were working at our Images of Christmas business, getting ready for a juried show. My niece, Misho, Ruth, and I had an established business creating Santa Claus figures. We designed for an international company and were invited to be the featured artists in Hanford's Showroom in the famous Peachtree Plaza of Atlanta, Georgia. Misho sculpted the faces and hands, and Ruth and I made the bodies and free cut the clothing. We used vintage quilts, raccoon coats, boiled wool, and antique accessories to complete our holiday vignettes. We were enjoying a busy season and considered our little business a success.

Just when our orders were completed for the season, a call came from one of my agents. She needed an arts-and-crafts instructor for a cruise out of Naples. Ruth had never been on a cruise, and was eager to go. We flew into Naples and were met by ship personnel who escorted us to the dock. The Mediterranean Sea is beautiful, and we were looking forward to going through the Straits of Gibraltar. I had cruised through the Straits of Gibraltar several years before with Maureen, headed for Fort Lauderdale. That time, the Mediterranean was so rough that passengers were confined to their cabins, so we never even saw the rocks of Gibraltar. Amazingly enough, as soon as we passed through the Straits and entered the Atlantic, thankfully the sea was like a mirror for the next five days of the crossing.

This time was different. Ruth and I were headed through the Straits and out to the Canary Islands. The ship docked at Gibraltar, and we signed up for an excursion to the top of the rock. We were enjoying the November weather in the south of Spain and wore only light jackets. There were many warnings about the wildlife.

The cable car ride to the top takes about six minutes and can hold up to thirty passengers. There is a large cement pad at the top for people to disembark and/or wait for the next car. The cable car ride unto itself is thrilling. Swinging high and higher as the car climbs, the views are breathtaking.

The 426-meter-high "rock" is home to the only wild monkeys on the European continent. The tailless Barbary macaques are everywhere and run free. Great caution is necessary walking the paths and watching the stone walls because they are numerous and everywhere. The macaques are not at all intimidated by people. Thankfully, they are also not overtly aggressive. Ruth and I kept reminding each other to watch where we walked, to remember to look down, to stay away from the macaques sitting on stone walls.

Sure enough, as we were on our way back to the cable car, I walked past a monkey who was waiting just for me. The back of my jacket was a lovely target, and his aim was perfect. Because of the balmy weather, I didn't put a shirt on under the jacket, so I couldn't take it off. Ruth has a weak stomach and an overactive gag reflex, so we made quite a sight, trying to cope with this messy situation before the car came to take us down the escarpment. As we were attempting to clean up, more and more people were gathering on the cement platform, until it was quite crowded. What had happened to me was very apparent and needed no explanation. Our walk through the dining room that night was slow, as people reached out with sympathetic greetings.

We really enjoyed the volcanic archipelago of the Canary Islands. We shopped in Arrecife and on Tenerife. A local artist was displaying his wares there, just outside an oceanfront cafe. After a great lunch, I bought two small oil paintings of local scenes, which I treasure to this day. The dazzling colors of Lanzarote, the easternmost island in the Canary chain, was spectacular. The black volcanic sand, the beautiful white houses, and the intense blue of the coral reefs make this one of the most beautiful places on earth.

Somehow Ruth talked me into riding a camel over those black sands. Now I know why camels are often muzzled. They are obnoxious creatures who hiss and spit with a vengeance. Like the donkeys in Santorini, I'm glad I did it. Thanks to Ruth and Pat for pulling me out of my comfort zone.

Images of Christmas life size figures of Mr. and Mrs. Santa Claus

Images of Christmas creation, "Looking for a Shorter Route"

# Casablanca, Taroudant, and Morocco

After Gibraltar and the Canary Islands, Ruth and I headed for Morocco. Just the name sounded dark and mysterious. Remember the movie *Casablanca* with Humphrey Bogart and Ingrid Bergman? It is still a romantic and iconic film. We were docking in Casablanca and spending two days there. We read and reread the brochures and attended the port lectures. There was so much to do and see, we couldn't wait. This was our first trip to Africa. Casablanca is the most important port in Morocco. It is the biggest artificial port on the planet and is protected by large jetties. It is a very busy commercial port as well as offering marina services, cruise ship harbors, and fishing fleet facilities.

We couldn't wait to shop the large souk, or bazaar. I bought my grandsons little (size two and four) real leather jackets there! They were adorable. The leather is of very high qualify, made from goat skin and tanned with sumac, making it very soft and pliable. The souk was everything we hoped for and more. Colorfully dressed "water men" in huge bejeweled hats strolled the streets, offering a drink of water from their tin cups. The outlandish costumes with bangles and beads caught the fire of the sun, and were constant reminders that we were indeed in one of the most exotic cities in the world. After the market, we went on the tour to Hassan II Mosque. That mosque is the largest in Morocco, the second largest in Africa, and the thirteenth largest in the world, so it was very impressive. The minaret is the tallest in the world at 210 meters, or 60 stories high. We enjoyed a full day in Casablanca.

Back on the ship, there were notes under our door inviting us to be "escorts" the following day on a bus trip to the walled city of

Taroudant. We were equipped with red umbrellas, and given instructions to take a head count on our buses before we left Casablanca and again before we left Taroudant. That was our only responsibility. There were local guides for us in Taroudant. The three-hour bus ride to the walled city and the Berber market was worth it. Taroudant was truly an oasis in the desert. The desert! We were en route to the Sahara Desert! On our way, the bus driver pointed out wild goats up in low bushy trees, eating the leaves. Goats who climb trees! This was truly an unusual place. Driven by a lack of food, these animals have adapted and with the aid of their sticky foot pads, have learned how to get to the top of the trees and more abundant leaves.

Taroudant is an orange, terra-cotta, gold-looking walled city near the foot of the Atlas Mountains. It is half oasis and half citadel. We were welcomed to the Riad Maryam restaurant with bottles of refreshing cold sodas and a chance to freshen up before an exotic and delicious lunch. I remember reading years later that the Duchess of York vacationed there often. A perfect, very private retreat, indeed. After lunch we proceeded to the market. The souk there is dark and scary. Our guide cautioned us to stay together and not stop to buy anything. The souk was indoors, with vendors separated by lengths of canvas. Making it even more claustrophobic, the stalls had canvas on the top, or ceiling, also. We walked single file, weaving our way through people and disappointed that we were unable to buy anything. I suppose this was to keep us together and manage the time, as we had a three-hour bus trip back. Shopping could have made this excursion way too long.

Stepping out into the bright Moroccan sun was a relief. I had recently begun taking pictures of youngsters on my travels, hoping to make a collection of children around the world. As we were walking back to the bus, I saw a young man of eight or nine, sitting with his father against a whitewashed wall. He was wearing a red fez—a perfectly composed picture. I motioned to the boy, then to my camera, and nodding and giving two thumbs up, was, I hoped, clear international sign language. The man nodded, and I began getting some great shots. After the first click of my camera, the man launched out of his chair and started running toward me. Frightened out of my mind, I began throwing dollar bills over my shoulder as I dashed for the bus with Ruth on my heels. Once we were each safely inside our buses, the man stationed himself just outside my window and glared at me until we took our head count and began the return trip to Casablanca.

All in all, the trip to Taroudant was unnerving. It remains in my memory as one of the most intimidating in all my travels. Now, some twenty years later, research paints a very different picture. Hotels abound, eclectic restaurants cater to developed palates, and excursions into the nearby Sahara Desert are very popular. It is truly an exotic place to visit.

# Hanging Out with a Sultanate

On one of our cruises early on, Angie and I were assigned a very eclectic table of six. The first couple was middle-aged and very conservative. The other couple totally transfixed us. He was dressed in a long robe and wore a turban-like head covering. She had beautiful sheer, sequined, and embellished scarves and flowing robes. The scarves concealed her hair and were twined over and around her neck. He introduced himself as the Sultanate of Oman, Fahid, and his wife, Fatima. When he said, "sultanate," I pictured lots of leaders from different regions, like our states, perhaps, with a sultan reigning over all. We looked forward to the conversations over dinner each night. After several meals together, we had become quite familiar. So familiar, that I asked if he knew a wonderful man from his country who would appreciate a good woman! We all got a good laugh out of that. But he expertly avoided answering my question.

Fahid's birthday was imminent, and he graciously invited us to join him in one of the cocktail lounges after dinner on his special day to celebrate. On the appointed evening, we enjoyed our dinner, savored our desserts, and then followed him and Fatima to one of the ship's lounges. There, he proudly produced a beautiful velvet bag, containing a bottle of Crown Royal whiskey. A waitress came to take our orders and when she saw the regal bottle in the middle of the table, politely informed Fahid that bringing your own libations was strictly not permitted in the lounges. He calmly nodded, and with a sweep of his hand indicated that we should order a beverage. When we all had a glass, he produced the whiskey and proceeded to top off each of our drinks. Angie and the other couple don't drink, and so

My Omani friends

Angie and Carol on the high seas

they were politely sipping his special and expensive Crown Royal, as we intoned toast after birthday toast to the sultanate.

Fatima abstained. I must admit to enjoying one drink of that rare elixir. Fahid punctuated the conversation with drink after drink until the bottle was almost empty. The waitress never bothered us! I whispered to Angie that we should leave very soon. I was certain that when Fahid stood up, he would fall over. Almost a whole bottle of Crown Royal! Unbelievable. We politely wished him a happy birthday once again and made our way to the door. The rest of the party followed, and Fahid walked and talked like he had been drinking ginger ale. That was an amazing demonstration and obviously not his first bottle of the Canadian blend!

We continued to enjoy their company every evening. On our last dinner together, Fahid invited us to visit him at any of Oman's Embassies—New York, London. He was going to New York next, but then would be back in Oman. We appreciated his warmth and hospitality and promised to look him up, if ever it were possible. He was *the* Sultanate of Oman. Expect the unexpected.

# The San Blas Islands

Maureen and I were on a cruise through the Panama Canal. It was hot and it was humid. We passed under the Bridge of the Americas at 7:00 a.m. It took all day to navigate the forty-eight miles of waterway into the Atlantic Ocean. The canal was fascinating as we passed through the locks. Between locks, the banks of the canal were lined with flora, fauna, mudbanks, and an occasional alligator. The most interesting port of call after the canal were the San Bias Islands. The San Bias Island archipelago stretches two hundred miles along the Panamanian Atlantic Coast. They are flat coral islands inhabited by the Kuna Indians. One morning we looked out our porthole and an indigenous Panamanian waved at us from his dugout canoe. I knew immediately this was going to be an exciting day. Getting off the tender at the crude dock, we watched in fascination as young lads speared flying fish and held them up for us to see. They really have wings! Their lateral fins are large and long and act as "wings." They can travel as fast as seventy miles per hour and can "fly" 160 feet, and up to 1,300 feet, with the aid of updrafts. It was a thrill to see them up close.

The village was very primitive, and the homes were thatched-roof bamboo huts. In the center of town there was a long structure on legs with a hinged wood arm set at an angle. Soon, a batch of sugarcane was placed on the horizontal surface and the angled board lowered to squeeze the sweet juice from the cane. A bucket caught this nectar as men took turns pulling the arm down on the cane.

As we walked through the village, we marveled at the intricate designs of the hand-stitched *molas* the Kuna are famous for. Several women were offering their wares as they rested under a palm tree.

They were dressed in mola blouses with scarves on their heads and gold rings in their noses and puffed on little pipes. Their legs were bound with bright beads from knee to ankle and were very, very thin. It reminded me of the bound feet of the Chinese women long ago. Some had parrots sitting on their shoulders while they stitched. The molas are multilayerd pieces of different colored fabrics intricately cut to form designs. The designs are taken from nature: like fish, parrots, plants, or even products of dreams and creative fantasy. The indigenous dress of the Kuna is one of the most spectacular in the Americas. Which puts them right up there in competition with the intricate weaving and embroidery of the Maya.

In this homogenized world, it is such a privilege to walk among an ancient culture still intact, living the life their ancestors led, clinging to the traditional ways. I was like a sponge, soaking this unique experience in. Lingering as long as we could, we bought lots of exotic molas with plans to make them into pillows, purses, yokes on dresses. In the last decade these native works of art have become quite popular. I have even seen mola pillows advertised in upscale and eclectic magazines. Now, twenty years later, I just embellished a denim jacket with some and made a purse for my grandson's wife. She was thrilled and honored that I shared them with her.

Back on the ship, the evening cocktail hour was spectacular as we sailed away with the sunset in the background of the glass atrium, topside. I was mingling among the guests, greeting some people who attended our classes, when an obviously affluent senior citizen struck up a conversation with me. "How did you enjoy your day?" I asked. And that began a tirade of unbelievable proportion. She was convinced the whole thing had been staged, that these Indians had been brought in for the day for our benefit. She did not buy any of those "tourist-trap cloths" and found the whole island disgusting. In the years I was cruising and working in Guatemala, the statistics were that 95 percent of the world lived exactly like those Kuna Indians and only 5 percent lived like we do. How unfortunate that some people never see the global picture. For Maureen and me it was one of those stellar experiences we'll never forget.

A Kuna woman displaying her molas

# A Lake in the Ocean

*A Lake in the Ocean.* That's what the brochure said, *A Lake in the Ocean.* I was poring over all the literature and excursion information I could get my hands on. Angie had again invited me to be her apprentice on a Caribbean cruise, starting in Barbados. The excursions all sounded wonderful. I wanted to walk on the same beach Columbus had explored on his first voyage. I wanted to eat a flying-fish sandwich. I wanted to tour the island, but what most intrigued me was "A Lake in the Ocean." Obviously, it was a trip to a sandbar where suddenly the water was only waist deep. The snorkeling was supposedly wonderful in the lake. Angie didn't swim, so she chose not to go. I set off at the appointed hour by myself.

The boat was old and wooden, wide and long. The captain was a tall young man in his twenties, lean muscled, ebony brown, and wore his French bathing suit well. His skin glistened in the sun and sea spray. The first mate was equally well endowed and very friendly. Most of the people on board were with a friend or a partner. Only two of us were traveling alone. When we arrived at our destination, the anchor was dropped and some cautionary instructions given before we entered the water. We were to stay on the starboard side of the boat, as the current was coming that way. In case of a problem, if you were on the starboard side, the current would carry you back to the boat. A sturdy set of wooden steps descended to the crystal-clear turquoise Caribbean.

I am a good swimmer and enjoy the water. However, having been mercilessly "dunked" during my teen years, I did have a fear of being underwater, especially against my will. Allowing my fellow passengers to go on ahead, I had plenty of time to observe their excitement as they swam among the schools of exotic tropical fish. Soon the boat was empty except for us two singles. As soon as my feet touched the sandy bottom, the current almost swept me away. I have never experienced such a strong rush of seemingly benign water. Fighting to stay calm and not panic, I immediately grabbed the ladder and started getting back in the boat. The first mate jumped into action, and came to my assistance. By this time, the other single woman was beginning to panic also. He assured us there was no need for concern, that he would take good care of us. He talked me back into the water, and proceeded to put our snorkel equipment on. In order to do this, because of the fierce current, he had one of us put our arms around him in the back, holding on tight, while he worked on the woman in front, then carefully moved us around until we were both ready. He gave each of us a hand and walked us around "the lake in the ocean" like we were pull toys.

The variety and abundance of fish was incredible. I forgot to be afraid I was so mesmerized by the amazing display of natural beauty. Soon my companion indicated that she was comfortable and wanted to go off on her own. This helpful young man continued to walk me around as I enjoyed the best snorkeling of my life. And then he pulled me up on my feet. Pointing at the sea, I was horrified to see a huge wave coming toward us. A wave over six feet high. Every fiber of my being went into panic mode. I was terrified, I held onto that first mate like my life depended on it, which I was convinced it did. I began to literally climb him in an attempt to stay on top of the water. He calmly put his hands on my waist and lifted me high over his head. His six foot plus head. The wave hit us, completely inundating him, while I watched it roll toward the boat. As he lowered me into the water once again, he thought it was his turn to climb me. Suddenly I realized my unbridled clutching and grabbing at his body had been misinterpreted. What was pure terror for me seemed like an invitation to him. Wow! After several emphatic *no, no, no* screams, he stopped and I snorkeled back to the boat.

What an experience! Angie hung on every word as I related my afternoon adventure to her.

# Angel Falls and the Orinoco River

I had been on cruises through the Caribbean many times and loved every minute on those crystal-clear, turquoise waters. When an agent called and ask me to do a cruise around the Caribbean and up the Orinoco River, I was thrilled. I immediately called Pat. She was as excited as I was. I always dreamed of going up the Amazon, but the Orinoco would be wonderful too. After the usual ports of call, we made our way south of the islands and were approaching the mouth of the Orinoco. After dinner, we climbed as high as we could get on the ship for a clear view of the sea and, hopefully, the river. We were not disappointed. Soon a ribbon of brown water was visible ahead, in stark contrast to the beautiful blue of the ocean. As we approached the brown stream, we realized this was the Orinoco River carrying eroded soil from up river out to sea.

As the ship turned into that brown water, it was a breathtaking moment. Almost literally breathtaking. The wind coming down stream was so hot and so strong, it almost did take your breath away. I had on a pant suit that buttoned down the front with lots of little covered buttons. Believe it or not, that wind almost blew my top right off. The buttons surrendered to the jungle, and I scrambled to get them closed and rebuttoned. It was like we were standing in front of a huge blast furnace. As dusk settled in, the jungle on each side of the boat came alive. Fires were visible along the shores, and villagers were moving through their evening routines. Pat and I were transfixed. This was Venezuela, South America. We could hardly believe it.

Before we left home, I tried to book an excursion to fly over Angel Falls, the highest waterfall in the world. The trip was entirely sold out. As soon as the excursion desk opened on the ship, I inquired again about the trip to Angel Falls. Completely sold out. I was so determined to experience that famous falls, that in the early morning of the day we docked in the head waters of the river, I jumped into some clothes and ran to the purser's desk, money waded up in my pocket. An elderly woman was ahead of me in line, trying to cancel her husband's excursion. The river was low because of a drought, and the ascent from the river up the bank to the road was steep. To assist with the climb, big equipment tracks had been put down, for the cleats to give people traction. The woman's husband could not navigate that. The purser explained that her only recourse was to sell the extra ticket. She didn't have to look far!

This trip was almost a whole day. We boarded a Venezuelan jet immediately and took off for Camp Canaima. After several passes over the breathtaking falls, we landed at the only clearing visible in the jungle. The "airport" building was four posts with a corrugated tin roof and some benches. This was the jumping off place for trekkers hiking up the falls. We had a lovely lunch followed by a few minutes in a little store where I bought my husband a blowgun! Interesting to see baby food, diapers, and blowguns all on the same shelf. Then the tour included a ride in a dugout canoe through the Canaima Lagoon. The lagoon was ringed by tall hills with flat tops, much like the mesas in our southwest. Indigenous people were bathing their children in the river, carrying water to their homes, and fishing in smaller canoes. This was a remarkable glimpse into another way of life. I couldn't believe my luck in getting a ticket at the last minute. My persistence paid off!

# The Inside Passage

Jane and her husband, Fred, were college friends. We enjoyed each other's company and visited often. When Jane heard I was cruising and cruising and cruising, she wondered how I could afford it as a single woman. When she found out how I was cruising, she became very interested and wanted to go with me sometime. When the opportunity came to sail the Inside Passage, Jane was excited. We flew into Seattle and took the high-speed train to Vancouver. The ship was beautiful, and our cabin was next to the Bridge couple who were also our companions in the dining room. Large windows in the dining room afforded everyone a view. Tables along the walls were under the windows. The rest of the dining room was elevated, allowing the middle of the room panoramic views as well. There's nothing like dining while watching a pod of whales cavort on the other side of the glass. I had been on this ship before with my niece, Misho, in the Mediterranean. There were many familiar faces, in the dining room, especially.

As we proceeded northward, we enjoyed all ports of call along the way. We shopped in Skagway, rafted down the Mendenhall River, and took a helicopter ride over the glaciers. In Juneau, we attended a Tlingit Indian cultural-center performance and went on a harbor cruise to see the sea lions and the tufted puffin. During that boat ride it began to rain, and we did not have rain gear or even hoods. In one of the shops I couldn't resist a beautiful reindeer hide. I had that strapped on my back as we trudged our way back to the ship. We really didn't realize how disheveled we looked until a car stopped and ask us for directions. "Oh my gosh, Jane—they thought we live here!" I said. We surely didn't look like the average tourist. It was about that time when Jane began to inform me repeatedly that she was missing her anniversary with Fred.

Every morning, Jane would say, "Only fifteen days until my thirtieth anniversary." "Only fourteen days until my thirtieth anniversary." And so on and so on and so on. I finally decided I better do something for this momentous occasion. I approached the meticulously groomed maître d' and requested an anniversary cake for Jane Dike on the anniversary evening. "Anniversary?" was the crisp reply. "But where is Mr. Dike?"

"Well, he's not on the cruise," I meekly replied. Evidently, this man had never heard of a woman vacationing during an anniversary by herself. Shaking his suave head in what seemed like sadness and disgust, he said, "Well, I dunno. I just dunno."

I left the dining room not knowing what would happen on Jane's big night. Finally, the big day arrived and Jane was pensive and subdued. She called Fred, and he didn't answer. She called again and left a message. She went into dinner in a rather somber mood. Just as we were enjoying our coffee, a parade of waiters burst upon the scene singing "Happy anniversary to you, happy anniversary to you!" When they got to us, total confusion registered on their faces. Where was the anniversary couple? The circle of men around us was enormous—most of the dining room. Many of them had recognized me and joined in the usual few waiters that served our table. They stopped singing. An awkward silence hung in the air. It was like someone sucked the air out of the dining room.

To bring some levity to the situation, I put my arm around Jane and said sweetly, "Oh, darling, isn't it wonderful to be out of the closet at last?" A glass-shattering "*Whoof*" came from the waiters as they started to breathe again and proceeded to do what they always do for anniversaries—tie the couple's wrists together with napkins as they resumed their song. By this time Jane was recovering from her initial shock. She was vigorously shaking her head back and forth, untied our wrists, and began chanting, "No, no, no!"

After that evening, Jane was careful to not walk too close to me, refused to share her umbrella, and would absolutely not even reggae with me. We managed to remain friends and continued to travel together. Now, we look back on that evening and laugh our heads off.

# Australia and Harry

My brother was a big help boxing up our Santas and modifying the workshop for us. He also became interested in my lack of a more exciting social life other than grandsons and Santa Claus. One weekend he and son, John, were guests at a local hunting club and got a brilliant idea. Becoming reacquainted with some local men they hadn't seen in a long time, one of them stood out. Harry Milhouse graduated from Benton High School one year after me. When we first moved to Benton in 1946, we lived in Harry's family cabin while our home was being renovated. I rode the bus home with Harry after school, and Harry's mother, Evelyn, babysat me until my parents closed the grocery store and picked me up each evening. Harry was in first grade; I was in second. Harry and I played in the hayloft, helped feed the calves, and had rollicking farm fun. Of course, all this was before Jim was born, but he knew the stories well. Harry had lost his wife several years before and was purportedly single. Jim and John thought I should meet him again. They thought he would be a perfect match for me. Harry lived in Washington, DC and worked for the Navy Department. He was also a realtor on the side. His brother still lived in Benton, and Harry owned several properties there. In fact, he tried to buy our family home from mother several years before. So we had lots of connections. The Vance "boys" couldn't wait to set us up.

We met over pizza one Friday night. John and wife Heather, brother Jim, and Ruth were in attendance, expecting to hear whistles blow and bells ring. Harry was spending the weekend in Benton. There was very little left in this man that I could recognize. I looked long and hard until I saw the glimmer in his eyes and listened to him talk. Slowly the young Harry came through. But there were no bells and whistles. He invited me out to dinner the next evening, and we had a marvelous time reminiscing and getting reacquainted. This former classmate had grown into a valued government employee, was witty, polished, and accomplished. We had fun together. We dated on and off for several months, took some trips in his motor home, and continued to get to know each other.

Then, one of my agents called and offered me a three-week trip to Australia. Australia! Wow! I always wanted to go to Australia. My friend Maureen always wanted to go to Australia. Now I had a big decision to make. My relationship with Harry had become a complicated one, and he was incredibly hard to read and very elusive in many ways. I was never sure where we were heading. After much deliberation, I decided that Australia would be a test. If a man saw no future in a relationship, then he surely wouldn't accept an invitation to spend a whole month 24-7 with someone he wasn't serious about. I wasn't suggesting marriage, we both professed to not want that, just a committed relationship. Something. Harry accepted my invitation, and we began making plans for this big trip. Things were looking up or so I thought.

I was amazed at how adept Harry was at leading totally separate lives in the confined quarters of a cruise ship cabin. We dined at our appointed table each evening, and that was the extent of our time together. We took different excursions, relaxed on different decks, made different friends. He was more trouble than he was worth at my classes, which I eventually dismissed him from. So the cruise was indeed a test. And Harry failed. Upon arrival home, I told him not to call, text, e-mail, or write. I never wanted to hear from him again. He ignored all those edicts, as was his nature, and he still contacts me now and then. And he did remarry, by the way—another former classmate from Benton High School. That was the glum side of the cruise.

Since we had flown into Sidney a few days before embarkation, we had time to see the major tourist attractions there. Sidney is the largest city in Australia. It is famous for its beautiful sand beaches, the famous Opera House, and the Harbor Bridge. The Opera House is a multivenue performing art center. It is one of the twentieth century's most famous and distinctive buildings in the world. It was designed by Jorn Utzon and completed by Peter Hall and an Australian architectural team. It opened in October 20,1973, after winning the International Design Competition. It commands Sidney Harbor. I remember eating incredible fish and chips out of a paper cone while strolling the grounds and listening to the haunting notes of the Aboriginal didgeridoo, a wind instrument now popular all over the world. The Sidney Harbor Bridge is the widest long-span Bridge and the tallest steel-arch Bridge in the world. It is also the fifth longest spanning-arch Bridge, according to the Guinness Book of World Records. Neither of us attempted to climb it, but one of my friends and fellow cruise itinerant, Jim Wood, did. He has a picture and a jacket to prove it!

The Great Barrier Reef was amazing and scary. The current was very strong, and only experienced swimmers and avid snorkelers were comfortable in the roped off area adjoining the observation platform. I was not among them. Content to watch from the safety of the excursion boat it was an amazing experience. The Great Barrier Reef is the world's largest coral reef system comprised of over 2,900 individual reefs and 900 islands stretching over 2,300 kilometers over an area of 344,4000 square kilometers. Located in the Coral Sea, off the coast of Queensland, Australia, it can be seen from outer space. It is the world's largest structure made by living organisms and was selected as a World Heritage site in 1981. I was beyond excited to be there and see this amazing phenomenon of nature.

We also docked in Cairns and Brisbane, as we cruised the east coast. Brisbane is the capital and most populated city in the state of Queensland and the third largest city in Australia. It has a population of approximately twenty-five million. We took a tour of the Blue Mountains and visited the Lone Pine Koala Sanctuary. The cities were like cities everywhere, but getting out into the country allowed us to see the real Australia.

After Australia, the cruise visited several South Pacific Islands, all of which I found fascinating. One sunny afternoon at sea, I was reading on one of the upper decks and noticed the sun was on my left. Several minutes later, when I came up for air, the sun was on my right! I couldn't figure out what was going on. We were on our way to Papua, New Guinea, and I was filled with anticipation. It was a wild land of blowguns and intrigue. A Rockefeller son had mysteriously disappeared there, years before. It was one of my most anticipated destinations. The captain interrupted my reverie with an urgent announcement. The ship had turned around. There was a cyclone bearing down on New Guinea, and it was necessary to change our itinerary.

Instead of Papua, our next port of call was Guadalcanal in the Solomon Islands. Guadalcanal is famous for the World War II battle that raged there from August 1942 to February 9, 1943. It was the first major offensive by the Allied Forces against the Empire of Japan. I booked an excursion into the jungle to see one of our fighter planes still suspended in the high jungle canopy. Sitting in our vehicle, a hush came over the forest as my fellow passengers and I imagined the bloody seven-month battle fought here. The courage, the fear, the lives lost, the pain. It all came through to me as I sat there, chills running through my body. It was an unnerving and almost traumatic experience. World War II is in the so distant past. This brought World War II right to our doorstep.

Our last island was Vanuatu, population 265,000. This tropical island was jointly administered by Britain and France until it gained independence in 1980. Our visit there was highlighted by a trip to a native village, a typical island lunch, and a folkloric performance by native dancers. The heat and humidity were oppressive. Just walking several steps, the temperature enveloped you. On the way back to the ship, I stopped to visit with some people sitting in the shade of a very large tree. Some of them were carving. I bought a beautiful oval bowl with an intricate seashell inlay around the rim. It is one of my treasures, and we use it frequently.

It was here that I booked an excursion on a seaplane. I was at the water's edge, watching as the six-seat Cessna smoothly glided over the water and came to a complete stop. The passengers hopped into the water and waded ashore. The pilot was in his fifties and a friendly fellow. He stopped to talk to me and asked if I was going up with him on the next trip. He invited me to join him up front for the next tour of the South Pacific Islands. I was delighted. I had never been on a seaplane. He collected tickets and then led me into the water and onto the plane. In line behind me were two couples. The first man had a plethora of things hanging from his neck. Binoculars, a huge camera with a variety of lenses, a smaller camera, extra film cases, etc. He was obviously agitated. With a heavy accent, he almost demanded that he sit in the front because he was taking pictures. "Oh, everyone is taking pictures," the pilot said calmly. With disgust, the man settled in the middle seat, grumbling under his breath.

It was a thrill to watch the pilot deftly maneuver the plane and fire up the engines as we skimmed over the water and then up, up and away we flew over the bluest of blue waters in this archipelago. With exaggerated strain, the obstreperous man with the cameras was groaning and grunting as he angled to get just the perfect shots. At the first lull, I produced my little disposable instamatic and started to also take pictures. It was like teasing a caged bull. The man evidentially had quite a temper, and he was having a hard time staying in his seat. The pilot winked and I winked back as we tried not to laugh out loud at this childish display.

# The Bucks County Organization
# for Intercultural Advancement

This organization needs a little explanation. It became a driving force in my life after I accepted a position on the board. When I attempted to resign after several years, I was elected president, which changed the direction of my life for the next ten years.

The Bucks County Organization for Intercultural Advancement (BCOIA) grew out of a group of adventurous educators in the Bucks County, Pennsylvania, Intermediate Unit in the early 1970s. During that time several chief school administrators from across the county traveled to Central America, South America, Africa, and the Middle East, consulting on curriculum, school design, and introducing new and innovative educational practices.

In the mid-1980s, Bucks County became affiliated with Dr. Robert MacVean, founder of the American School of Guatemala, a private, coeducational, bilingual day school and the University of the Valley of Guatemala, which was an outgrowth of the American School experience. Dr. MacVean needed native English speakers for his bilingual K–12 program and US trained professors for the university programs in the natural sciences. Guatemalan law restricts the hiring of foreigners, so the help of an outside organization was needed to obtain visas and administer the payroll.

MacVean approached Bucks County in Pennsylvania and asked them to sponsor programs at the American School and the University of the Valley. Bucks County agreed, and in 1986, Dr. MacVean was able to register Bucks County as an International Mission with the Ministry of Foreign Relations. Acceptance by the Ministry provided the necessary courtesy visas. In 2004, the Ministry of Finance also recognized the Bucks Organization, allowing BCOIA to administer payroll and other funds within Guatemala as a tax-exempt international mission. Dr. MacVean, working out of an office at the Universidad del Valle, was the first representative of Bucks County in Guatemala. With the Finance Ministry approval, an independent local office has been established, and Mrs. Barbara Baker Barillas was named Bucks County representative for Guatemala.

Currently, BCOIA sponsors approximately 125 educators in Guatemala, 77 of whom are visiting teachers at the American School (Colegio Americano de Guatemala, or CAG) and 11 of whom are BCOIA fellows at the University of the Valley (Universidad Valle de Guatemala). In addition, payroll services have been extended to another school—Interamericano de la Montana de Guatemala, a K–12 school modeled on the American School. Mrs. Barillas assumed the post of local representative for BOCIA, following her retirement as Director of the American School in June, 2005. Since that time, BCOIA has initiated several programs which bring the involvement of the organization and the schools in Guatemala even closer. UVG and CAG have sponsored satellite schools, one in the highlands, the Altiplano, and one on the south coast, the Proesur.

The Altiplano was a former military base during the civil war. When the war was over, the government sold the installation to the American School and established a college there. Barracks became dormitories and open fields became agricultural projects. BOCIA took this facility under their umbrella and provided them with educational materials as well as guest speakers and educational seminars during our annual visit. It was very emotional to see teachers who had come on a chicken bus, riding through the night to attend these seminars and accept materials for their classrooms.

As president of BOCIA, I was very excited to attend the graduation of the first class at the Altiplano and watch these rural people receive a degree in higher education that had been impossible for them when the only colleges and universities were far away in Guatemala City. Families attended dressed in their finest native garb—a cacophony of colors as the clothing of different villages

Guatemalan school girls at the Altiplano School

mixed and mingled. School children performed. Choirs sang. Photos were taken. Food was served. It was truly a day that would go down in the history of this Third World country. A tiny step forward. A big step in public education.

The Proesur had been established years before to provide education to the families of the sugarcane workers. It is a beautiful complex of classrooms and enjoys a dedicated staff. We were always welcomed with great anticipation and our educational seminars were well received. The children greeted us with musical programs and delighted in sharing their projects with us. The teachers there were happy to introduce us to some of the public schools in the area, because they were woefully understaffed and had virtually no educational supplies.

One "school" was a corrugated tin roof on four poles, bamboo walls, and several very old chairs. To have BCOIA board members visit with tablets, pencils, crayons, books, etc. was like getting mana from heaven. In anticipation of our visits, parents would accompany their children to school to express gratitude for our help. Again, in our honor, they were always dressed in their finest and resplendent Mayan clothing. These visits were emotional. My husband was so moved at this school that he had to walk away until he could get himself under control. This was truly gratifying work, and we always returned home with renewed energy to continue to gather materials and donations for the next visit. We were making a difference in education in the public schools of Guatemala.

Some of these trips turned out to be more interesting than others. I was deeply involved in planning our next trip to Guatemala, when a friend stopped in to visit. She was a realtor and had just come from a restaurant/bar near Williamsport. The owner wanted to list his property. He was Guatemalan! She couldn't believe it. Of course, we got to know this gentleman over many months, and coincidentally, he was also planning a trip to Guatemala in the spring. One of my biggest hurtles in planning these visits is transportation. It is not readily available unless booked in advance and quite pricey. Naturally, we tried to keep the cost down as much as possible for board expenses. And we always wanted to do a little exploring after our BOCIA business was over and we were on our own.

Over dinner one evening, Carlos announced that he would be in Guatemala the same time we would be there. I gave him the name of our hotel and we arranged to meet for breakfast at the end of our official stay. He brought a friend with him, the former police chief of Guatemala City! He had a car and Carlos's aunt had given him the use of her lake house in Panajachel right on Lake Atitlan. We were invited to spend a few days at his aunt's house. Chief Juan and Carlos would stay in town. That sounded like a fine idea to the remaining board members.

Travel in the country can be a little dangerous because Guatemala was still involved in a civil war. Traveling with a Guatemalan and the retired police chief gave us a sense of security. The house was large and beautiful, had a caretaker, guardian, and was right on the lake. The men moved us in and we all went out to dinner. The next day it was so much fun traveling with these guys. They helped negotiate purchases, carried our packages, and maintained a running narrative of the lake, the villages, the people. Taking a risk very often affords wonderful experiences that one would never have otherwise. Of course, common sense and discretion are the operative words here.

# Adventures on Vacation

# Come Home

In due time the geese fly high
They grace the sky in flight.
Winging intent upon their destination
Seeing them, I'm seeing you,
A part of that formation.
In your due time, wing your way home
Where home is just not
The same without you.

—Jenet Watters Vance 1991

# Costa Rica

During my time in Central America, and after I returned to Pennsylvania, I was able to take several trips that did not include cruising. I enjoyed the company of friends and family and continued my quest to "see it all"!

One of my best traveling companions remained Pat Marino. She and I took that wonderful cruise through the Mediterranean and the Black Sea right before I went to Guatemala, so naturally, she was anxious to visit me after I got settled in there. We were able to coordinate her visit and the end of my first semester at the American School. We planned a week in Guatemala followed by a trip to Costa Rica and then both of us flying back to Pennsylvania together. I was living in Antigua in my little apartment with the tiny guest room, and we had a wonderful time hitting all the big tourist spots in Guatemala. While we were there, Pat experienced her first little earthquake. It is disconcerting to feel "the earth move under your feet!" Then, all too soon, it was time to visit Costa Rica.

The Latin culture is very accommodating. There is a strong desire to please. There is also a strong desire to be as modern and electronic as the first world. I had a bank account in Guatemala City and a debit card. Because US currency is widely accepted in Costa Rica, I wanted US dollars. I had just received my travel-allowance check from the American School and I intended to use that to finance my trip. After discussing my plans with a bank clerk, he assured me the check would clear by the following day, and the funds would be available. So instead of cashing the check, I deposited it in my account so that I could use my debit card during this vacation.

That gave my bank balance the boost it would need to keep me solvent and my balance in the black. Or so I thought.

I put my plane ticket on the debit card. I withdrew travel money and paid for tours and the hotel with my debit card. We arrived in San Jose without incident. San Jose is a delightful city about 1,200 meters above sea level. Costa Rica is located in the isthmus of Central America bordered by Panama and Nicaragua. There are several volcanoes, fruitful plantations, and dense rain forests. Our hotel was a mini-museum, housing beautiful artifacts and local art. After careful consideration, we decided our five days would be best spent by taking tours, rather than exploring on our own as we loved to do.

We spent the first day driving to the Pacific coast, visiting a rain forest on the way. Our guide was a professor at the University of Costa Rica. The professor led us deep into the forest, pointing out frogs and bugs along the way. I asked if there were howler monkeys here. "Oh, yes, many of them." he replied. I wondered if he could call them. "As a guide, I am not allowed to disturb them, but you can call them if you want to!" he said. Making the call of the howler monkey had become my new skill and entertaining friends with my jungle expertise was often requested. We all stopped our trek as I threw back my head and did the *Ooh, ooh, ooh, ooooh* call. My travel companions looked at me like I was demented. They evidently had never heard such sounds come out of an otherwise seemingly demure lady. *Oooh, ooooh, ooh, oooh*, came the answering call. They were there! Using their sound as a beacon, we were able to see them, expertly camouflaged in the tropical canopy. Binoculars brought them into sharp focus, and the entire group was thrilled to have seen and heard these elusive residents of Central America. Back on the road, it was a good thing we were all wearing sunglasses because halfway to the coast, the windshield exploded, shooting glass shards all over the van. We completed the trip sans windshield, and it was repaired while we had lunch and experienced the Pacific coast.

Our most enjoyable tour in Costa Rica was an overnight to the Atlantic coast. We traveled by van over the spine of mountains that run through Central America to a dock where we boarded an old double-deck boat. Chugging up the Tortuguero Canal, we saw caimans, turtles, monkeys, and osprey. Suddenly, the Caribbean Sea was dead ahead. Surely, we weren't heading right out into the open water? At the very last moment, the boat turned into a hidden canal and proceeded to our Botel. The rooms were very bare bones—with two single beds and a chair. The dining hall was a large screened-in building across a clearing. We were smack dab in the middle of the jungle. Pat went on a hike to the top of a hill where the view was spectacular. I took a john boat ride up a little stream further into the jungle and saw alligators, monkeys, and lots of birds. Back in the city, we toured lemon and banana plantations, volcanoes high in the cloud forest, and all the city of San Jose had to offer. It was a wonderful trip.

Upon our return to Guatemala City, we stayed with a friend before traveling together back to Pennsylvania. We were in line at the airport waiting to board our flight when things began to unravel. I had two huge bags and a very beautiful double-framed painting by Mchirix Stottz of Comolapa, Guatemala, packed in a hand-woven bag used to take avocados to market. The painting was well wrapped and padded with clothing, and I intended to gate check it. Suddenly, a uniformed policeman approached me and asked for my passport. After reading my name, he asked me to follow him. Puzzled and upset, I left Pat and my bags and went with him to a kiosk in the middle of the concourse. There, a woman who pretended to speak no English showed me a note from the bank. I was overdrawn! What! I had been so careful to not exceed my budget.

How could this happen? Until I could make restitution, I would not be allowed to leave the country. Reluctantly, I took out my American Express card and she called it in. (Scanning cards in 1991 was not possible.) The phone rang busy. She hung up. I gave her a MasterCard. Same deal. By now nervous perspiration was dripping off my earlobes. Curling her lips into a sneer, this unsympathetic Spanish-speaking person leaned into my face and shouted, "Forrrrrget about yourrrr trrrrreeep!"

I raced back to the gate where people were now boarding the plane and grabbed Pat. She gave this gracious ambassador to Guatemala one of her cards, and thankfully it went through. We were the last two passengers on the plane and just in time for me to see my beautiful oil painting flying through the air like a Frisbee. Careless baggage handlers were ignoring the "fragile" stickers I had plastered all over the woven bag. As I walked down the aisle of the plane, passengers were smiling, stroking my hand, and offering kind words, obviously relieved that I had made it aboard. It's not every day that you see a fellow passenger being taken out of line in a foreign country by local police. That's pretty scary stuff.

Fortunately, my Stottz painting arrived intact with only a few dents in the frame. That whole situation was caused because the check I deposited a week prior had still not cleared! Guatemala is, after all, a Third World country. I should have known.

# Saint Thomas, US Virgin Islands

Joan, my Guatemala hostess, and I remained good friends after I returned to the states. Joan spent the winter months with her daughter in Saint Thomas. Ingrid and husband, Dick, owned several shops on the island, and Joan helped them wherever she could. In later years, Ingrid didn't want to leave Joan alone while they attended an annual trade show in Germany. So guess what? She called me and asked if I would come down and keep her mother company. It was really tough duty, but I persevered. I persevered for ten years! We had wonderful times together. I was encouraged to invite a friend, which I did several times. Both Angie and Maureen joined us through the years. We traversed that whole island in Ingrid and Dick's car. One year, they left us with a brand-new model. It had six miles on it when I arrived. Joan and I didn't want to know how many miles were on it when I left.

We traversed Saint Thomas as well as the nearby island of Saint John, with regularity. What a wonderful way to spend a few weeks in the winter! The house was on a bluff overlooking the harbor and the capital of Charlotte Amalie. Waking up in the morning, merely opening your eyes afforded one a view of the harbor and the cruise ships coming in for the day. The house was beautifully furnished with island decor and Guatemalan antiques. A wide terrazzo terrace ran the whole width of the house, which was all glass. In other words, our accommodations were magnificent. Over the years, we took a launch to Virgin Gorda, flew to Saint Croix, and sailed on the famous *True Love* from the film *High Society*. The island is full of wonderful restaurants, and we did a good job of sampling most of them.

Joan visited me in Benton, Pennsylvania, and delighted in meeting my son and family. My grandsons, Austin and Ethan, took to her immediately and patiently showed her how to fish in their pond. My son, Scott, took us in his four-wheel drive SUV up through the high pasture to see a newborn fawn. Our area had a large deer population, and Joan loved to go "spotting" them at dusk. Friends took us high up on Red Rock Mountain to a private hunting lodge for an afternoon of riding all-terrain vehicles. My brother and Ruth entertained her at their Bloomsburg Fair stand where they were baking their famous homemade apple dumplings. Joan got a grand tour of Columbia County.

Years later, Bob and I were traveling in our motor home, and we visited Joan in Texas. She and Ingrid and Dick had retired in a beautiful Sun City development. As usual, Joan was involved in all kinds of activities. She was learning to tap dance, taking art lessons, and belonged to a Bridge club. She was still interviewing people, and filled us in on several of her neighbors.

The house in Saint Thomas was on the market. Over dinner one night, Ingrid and Dick urged us to go down and stay for a few weeks. They were very serious and would actually appreciate someone being in the house. What an incredible idea! We ultimately accepted this generous offer. In fact, we even became engaged there! Watching the iguanas in the treetops just beyond the terrace and enjoying the sunset over the Caribbean was our favorite end of-the-day activity. I have a soft spot in my heart for Saint Thomas.

Joan and Carol in Texas

# Africa

Soon after I retired and moved back into our family home in Benton, Pennsylvania, my bedside phone startled me out of a delicious morning sleep. Who could be calling me so early? Half-awake, half-disturbed, half-annoyed, I reluctantly picked up the phone. My brother began the conversation without so much as a good morning. Instead he rushed into a dialogue so fast and with such excitement I couldn't keep up. As I woke up and he slowed down, I began to understand that he had heard something about a trip to Africa on the morning news. Very affordable, all inclusive, photo safari to Kenya. He delivered the information staccato style without coming up for air. "Get on it," he ordered. The morning show didn't give specifics, and he didn't even know the airline or travel agent.

By now I was wide awake and getting excited. Africa! Beyond my wildest dreams. My brother, Jim, is very selective about how and where he vacations because he is self-employed. Time off is time without pay. But he was willing to take two weeks off to go on safari. I was retired and always ready to go anywhere!

I snuggled back down into the warm bed, closed my eyes, and turned on my search engine. I do my best thinking in bed. How to find out about this trip mentioned on the morning news? It wasn't an advertisement, but a public-service announcement informing the viewers that Africa is now affordable. Well, why not just call NBC? The trip was being offered by British Air, with a night flight to London, and then another night flight to Nairobi. In just a few hours I had a travel agent working on it, getting times, dates, and itineraries. My brother, Jim, wife Ruth, daughter, Misho, and I were booked on a fall trip to Africa.

The next few weeks were spent renewing passports, getting the required immunizations and packing, packing, packing. Formal dress was required for our stay at the prestigious Safari Club at the base of Mount Kilimanjaro, but most of the trip required outdoor clothing, hiking boots, and photographers' vests. Our first night was spent in the beautiful and exclusive Windsor Club outside Nairobi before we traveled into the bush. There, we met our guide, Fred, and were given general information on the entire excursion and encouraged to experience downtown Nairobi the next day.

We traveled in a game-viewing van that held eight passengers with a roof that opened to allow tourists to stand while safely viewing game and taking pictures. The other couple was from Vermont, had never been out of New England, and had won the trip at a Taco Bell! Our last companion was a young psychologist from Denver who commanded attention and regaled us with stories about her "Daddy" and "Mommy." The passenger seat next to Fred was usually empty. I found out why soon enough. We whine and complain about small potholes and uneven pavement on our paved and divided highways, but they are nothing compared to the roads in Kenya. Tour vans, buses, and huge tractor trailers vie for dominance on the pitted and pocked treacherous byways of this country. Fred deftly navigated the smoothest route he could over and around these sometimes crater-like holes. He invited each of us in turn to sit in the passenger seat up front next to him. Riding up there was not for the faint of heart. After the first dose of "riding shotgun," many of us did not repeat the experience.

Before we departed, my son, Scott, told me about an article he read about elephants. They are intelligent animals, communicate with each other, have rather developed memories, and even grieve at the loss of a loved one. He said a full tour van like we would be traveling in, came up on a dead baby elephant, with the mother anxiously standing vigil. She repeatedly started off to follow the herd, only to circle back when her baby didn't follow. Awed by this drama, the tourists watched in fascination as the mother tried and tried to get her offspring up and running. Finally, Mama realized the baby was dead and went into a rage. She headed for the tour van, flipped it on its side and stomped on it until the bus and contents were as flat as a squashed tin can. There were no survivors. Beware of those huge creatures and don't come between a baby and its mother, Scott cautioned.

One evening after dinner, Jim approached a guard and asked about the possibility of the four of us going on a little night drive. Nocturnal game viewing is highly frowned on, in order to give the animals some solitary time without tourists in their midst. However, the guard, eager to please, agreed to pick us up at dark. We drove into the bush where powerful spotlights soon picked up a herd of elephants. There were young calves among them. Yikes—just what Scott told me to avoid. The drive went without incident, but did give me an adrenaline rush until we were safely back on the road.

Each day started with a game drive, followed by wonderful breakfasts and ended with a game drive at dusk, followed by incredible dinners. We traversed most of Kenya, stopping at the national parks where special excursions were scheduled. At one of them, we met a rhinoceros who had been raised in captivity and was very docile. It was a thrill to be able to get up close and personal with such an amazing example of evolution defied. His handler assured us he was like family and the stout hearted among us were welcome to touch that thick, wrinkled, prehistoric hide.

Miss psychologist was the first to approach the beast's rear quarter and tentatively reached out a timid hand to feel his ample posterior. Suddenly this huge creature hosed her down with an incredibly healthy stream of steaming urine. *From behind.* Now wait a minute. I needed an explanation for this phenomenon. Everyone knows how every animal, including humans, relieve themselves and this demonstration was not like anything we had ever seen or read about. "How did he do that?" I asked our guide.

"Well, miss, de penis, she swings to de front and she swings to de back."

Ruth and Misho were staring at the ground and had stopped breathing. My brother's eyes had disappeared into his head, and his face was a brilliant scarlet. I know he was praying I would stop this line of questioning, but the ramifications of this unusual feat were dancing around in my head. How do they mate? How do they decide to water things in the front, compared to things behind them? Or can they only mate in the front and urinate out the back? Meanwhile, our very wet fellow tourist was trying to cope with her saturated safari attire and regain her composure. Research proved this information to be correct. In fact, the urinary equipment of this animal has been described as a fire hose that has a trajectory of nine to thirteen feet. It is meant to mark their territory. The defecation process is equally as unusual, and involves a fast spinning of the tail—but I'll let that research up to my dear readers.

Our senses were bombarded all along this enlightening odyssey. From the bawdy Third World cacophony of Nairobi, to the splendor of Mount Kenya and its show-stopping, world-class Mr. Kenya Safari Club, the wonder of the dark continent titillated me as only the wild and off-beat places in this world can. Driving north on the main highway to Ethiopia, we passed Somalians, Ethiopians, and Arabs, along with the Kenyan tribes of the Kikukus, Turkanas, and Maisi.

For me, this was the real Africa, the mysterious East as I had imagined it would be. Observing the diversity of intricate neck-pieces, headgear, body wraps, skin color, all interwoven with the daily activities of tending goats, gathering firewood, collecting rain-water, selling local produce, to bartering and trading for necessities. All these illustrate the disparity between our cultures. Life goes on here as usual in exotic sounding places like Maroa, Isiolo, Nanuki. Every year the world gets smaller and more homogenized. All over the world, thousands more native peoples adopt western dress and leave the old ways behind. Will my grandchildren or their children be privileged to experience a native culture, or understand their own place in civilization by walking among those from a different one?

The high points of this trip were indeed watching a maned lion feed on his kill, the mighty elephants shield their young from our eyes, the sinuous descent of a leopard from his high perch in an aca-cia tree, and the rollicking good time had by all in the hippo pool. Yes, I'll always remember the silent tread of animals just beyond the ring of light at Sweetwater Camp, the spotted hyena rolling in his mudhole, and the frequent and comical hither-and-thither dartings of the warthog. Herds of zebra punctuated sunsets over the Masai Mara and rolling hills announced the beginning of the Serengeti Plain. But deeper than this, under it all, was the heady glimpse into Africa as it was, as it is, as it is struggling to remain. The Africa of the Samburu and the Kikuku and the Masai.

Contrasting this trip with my Guatemala experience has given me some insight into what I really enjoy and what my real focus is. In Guatemala, there were few wild animals, but the beautiful people were the source of wonder and delight. In Africa, of course, the animals are the attraction, not the people. However, after a week at home, I found that it was still the people that captivated me, with the animals adding excitement and color to the wonder we call Africa. It was very exciting to see the tribes and nationalities mixing together to weave a complex cloth of the Eastern Kenya desert communities. The fight for human survival in a hostile environment moved me more than the herds of elephant and pools of hippopotami. The land of Jambo, Karibou, Hakuna Matata, and Asanta sana is a world away, but the memories are vivid and real. A stellar chapter in a life-well lived.

Samburu warriors in Kenya

My niece, Misho and the amazing rhinoceros

# Vacationing in the Dominican Republic

My friends, Jane and Fred owned a time share. During one of my visits to their home, they were looking for a new place to use their vacation weeks. We had a long history of traveling together, and it was their turn to plan our winter break. After some research, we decided on a few weeks in the Dominican Republic for the coming winter. We settled on a property on the north shore in the seaside town of Cabarete. The resort was all inclusive and provided all-day shuttle service from the hillside location down to Sosúa Beach. It looked perfect.

Jane and Fred flew down from New England, and I joined them from Pennsylvania in the capital city of Santo Domingo for a few nights before we proceeded to Cabarete. Our stay in Santo Domingo was delightful. The town square was hosting a folkloric festival with vendors, music, and dance. Restaurants served Caribbean food alfresco, and we visited a larimar and an amber factory, two semiprecious gems the island is famous for. We toured the Christopher Columbus house and museum and several beautiful and very old churches. The arched brick ceilings and symmetrical columns and architecture were amazing.

Then we took a bus to the north shore of this island nation and settled into an absolutely beautiful suite high atop a hill overlooking the Caribbean Sea. Under our balcony, the land slipped away into a breathtaking tapestry of lush and vibrant tropical plants. This profusion of vegetation was held back by one of three pools and an amphitheater. The vibrant blooms were a feast for the weary eyes of winter travelers from the northeast in the middle of January.

We loved Sousa beach. Under a thick row of palm trees for at least five hundred yards, vendors proudly displayed beautiful pieces of art, pottery, clothes, material, carvings, and even food. Then there was a strip of sunny sand and then the beautiful blue water. It offered everything. Sun, shade, shopping, snacking, dining, swimming. The north shore was also famous for kite or wind surfing. The sky over the beach was a rainbow of beautifully colored kites soaring along on the coastal winds. We began to routinely spend the day enjoying all Cabarete had to offer. And we slowly began to meet other people vacationing in the Dominican. It proved to be a very interesting group of people.

The hotel was organizing an excursion to ride horses on a stretch of beach nearby. We signed up. In our small group there was a tall, handsome lawyer from Texas, two women from England, a young couple on their honeymoon, and two guys from Russia, who spoke no English and kept to themselves, until they got on horses, that is. Galloping far ahead of the group, suddenly, they turned back toward us and leaped up on their saddles. Whooping and hollering, they did what was essentially a circus act right there on that unpopulated stretch of sand. We were speechless. I forgot my anxiety about riding a horse and watched this amazing performance. When it was over, these acrobats became introspective once more, like someone had thrown a switch, retreating into their own world and quietly sipping the Russian vodka they brought with them.

Guests were constantly checking in and out of the resort, and so every day was a different parade of people. One lazy afternoon, Jane and I were relaxing by the pool, and Fred was reading and dozing. The Russians were playing chess, and the lawyer, Tom, was sunbathing. Suddenly, a dozen or so people came through the office and walked past the pool on the way to their accommodations. The men had huge professional video cameras on their shoulders, and the women were all beautiful, voluptuous and scantily dressed.

By now, we had gotten to know Tom, and after the parade passed, we put Tom on it! Find out what these people are here for, and where they came from. Last week he reported that the Russians were, indeed, circus performers. Now he had a new assignment. Very soon some of the newcomers returned and jumped into the pool. We had never seen bathing suits like the women wore or weren't wearing, maybe. Fred lost interest in his book and was suddenly wide awake. The women started a rousing game of water basketball, which involved much jumping, jiggling, bouncing, and screaming. Jane had to help poor Fred turn his book right side up.

The attire for dinners was equally as fascinating. In the early nineties, we had never seen shorts that ended before the derriere did, or transparent blouses with strategically placed pockets. Good old Tom came through again. Turns out this was a film crew from Hungary here to film a pornographic movie. They had rented a secluded house down the beach, and only a few worked on any given day, leaving the rest to cavort in the pool and in the sea. Fred really loved Cabarete and this wonderful time share. He especially loved to spend his afternoons poolside reading and enjoying a cool libation, watching basketball games. Basketball had become Fred's new interest, to Jane's consternation!

The waters off the coast of the Dominican are the breeding grounds for a high percentage of our planet's whales. We decided we should go on a whale watching trip. It was an all-day trip, starting early, stopping for breakfast, and then proceeding to the bay off the north coast where the whales were breeding.

On the way there, because we were going on a big boat, I was relating the experience some of my fellow outdoor writers had viewing whales off the coast of California. A small boat of tourists the day after their excursion was overturned by a huge whale, and everyone drowned. When we arrived at the water, the double—decker boat we had booked was waiting—but it was full. We were relegated to a small boat with a pubescent teen as the captain. We set out for the viewing area, and my friends asked me with trepidation in their voices if the whales were put off by the sound of the outboard motor. Oh yes, I assured them, just as the motor stalled and we were dead in the water. Then, a whale head appeared. Just the head. It was standing upright in the sea, just looking at us. Staring at us. I must admit to getting a shiver down my spine. It was eerie. It was scary. Jane and Fred were terrified. A patrol boat monitoring the area pulled up beside us and boarded our boat. We passed his inspection, the whale disappeared, and we safely docked on an island for lunch and relaxation.

The two weeks flew by. We made plans to return the following year. Cultural enlightenment, historical facts, abject terror, and titillation, all rolled into one vacation. Who wouldn't want to return?

# Facing Retirement

I signed on for a third year at the American School with one provision. I would terminate my contract and return home immediately if anything happened to my mother. When I made this request, mother was seventy-seven and in relatively good health, but I was becoming concerned that I was away too long during her golden years. And I was concerned about facing retirement.

Before my marriage was over, I had begun to write cookbooks on the preparation of wild game. I was ultimately invited to join Outdoor Writers of Pennsylvania and Outdoor Writers of America. I produced four cookbooks and had articles published in several magazines. I was on the masthead of *Pennsylvania Game News*. I gave all that up when I went to Guatemala. Now, I was only fifty-five and still had lots of energy. After being a principal, I didn't think I wanted to go back into a classroom. I didn't think I was ready for full retirement, however.

As it turned out, I didn't have to make any decisions. I was in my office at the American School one afternoon when my phone rang. It was my brother. Mother was in an ambulance on the way to the hospital. That was all he knew, but he suspected she had had a stroke. I was living in Antigua and riding a bus to and from school. The call came about two and the bus left at three. I was on the next flight out in the morning.

Mother had indeed suffered a stroke and passed away five days later. I got to her bedside in time for her to know I was home safe and sound. So retirement was not exactly a choice. I was living in my childhood home in the little town of Benton, Pennsylvania, and enjoying the company of family and two wonderful little grandsons. For Christmas that year, I made every family a Santa Claus figure designed to match the decor of their houses. My sister-in-law, Ruth, was very excited. She and her daughter, Misho, and I had been looking for some kind of business venture. "This is it! This is it!" Ruth exclaimed. "This is our business." Our company, Images of Christmas, was born that night. And that was how our business of making Santa Claus figures began.

My retirement activities were no longer a concern. I also became a hands-on grandma and enjoyed being part of my grandson's lives. My Benton years were full of family, Santas, and substitute teaching. Just as the boys were starting to drive, ready to begin their own adult lives, a miracle happened. My high school sweetheart came back into my life.

Misho got married, I got married, we closed the Images of Christmas shop, and I retired for good this time. My husband, Bob, and I moved to a beautiful lake in South Carolina, and we are enjoying our golden years in the Southern sun. It was with his urging that I wrote all these adventures down. And I bet I've missed some. Writing this book has allowed me to experience all my amazing memories all over again, from the comfort of my office. It's been quite a journey. I am truly blessed.

Carol Vance Wary, author of Wild Game Cookery

Carol with second husband, Bob Edwards, in their
pergola on Lake Marion, South Carolina

# About the Author

My life did a complete turn-around when my high school sweetheart walked back into it. After being alone for nineteen years, suddenly I had a partner. I never stopped loving the handsome, kind, and talented boy I was so attracted to when we were young. I was in shock, really, that this kind of thing could happen. Bob joined me teaching on cruise ships, supported my philanthropic work with the public schools in Guatemala, and shared my enthusiasm for life. We went on wonderful trips in his motorhome. No more shoveling snow for us! Winters were spent traveling throughout the South and then eventually renting homes during the winter months. Our favorite Southern destination was the St. Johns River in Central Florida. While we were there, we bought a boat and enjoyed the plethora of wildlife that inhabit that river system. We even got married on our boat in a secluded lagoon that looked like something out of *The African Queen*. It has been a wild and crazy ride. I don't think I fully appreciated what a rich and full life I have had until I began writing this tome. It has been so much fun reliving each chapter as I wrote them. I want to thank my husband again and again for urging me to do this. When I began, I had no idea what a daunting task it would become. But I know it was worth all the time, reams of paper, and ribbons of ink. I believe everyone should write their personal story in order for those that come after will be able to see you, not just as the funny old lady, "Auntie Carol," or as the elderly relative who likes to carve and make furniture called "Uncle Bob," but as the young and vital people we were throughout our lives and still are—on the inside!

CPSIA information can be obtained
at www.ICGtesting.com
Printed in the USA
BVHW021340190122
625950BV00005B/88